THE CONFIDENCE TRICK

The City's Progress
From Big Bang To Great Crash

THE CONFIDENCE TRICK

The City's Progress
From Big Bang To Great Crash

BY

CHARLES JENNINGS

HAMISH HAMILTON · LONDON

HAMISH HAMILTON LTD

Published by the Penguin Group
27 Wrights Lane, London W8 5TZ, England
Viking Penguin Inc, 40 West 23rd Street, New York, New York 10010, U.S.A.
Penguin Books Australia Ltd, Ringwood, Victoria, Australia
Penguin Books Canada Ltd, 2801 John Street, Markham, Ontario, Canada L3R 1B4
Penguin Books (N.Z.) Ltd, 182–190 Wairau Road, Auckland 10, New Zealand

Penguin Books Ltd, Registered Offices: Harmondsworth, Middlesex, England

First published in Great Britain 1988 by
Hamish Hamilton Ltd

1 3 5 7 9 10 8 6 4 2

British Library Cataloguing in Publication Data
Jennings, Charles
  The confidence trick.
  1. London (City). Financial institutions.
  Deregulation
  I. Title
  332.1-09421-2

ISBN: 0241-125-227

Typeset in 11/13 pt Palatino
Printed and bound in Great Britain by
Richard Clay Ltd, Bungay, Suffolk

To Susie

CONTENTS

PREFACE

The Confidence Trick is a book with three subjects: the tribalism peculiar
to the City of London; the City's bubble-like reliance on mere ideas for
its business; and the City's disorientating ethical habits. It was conceived on Black Monday, and finished some six months later. You get
caught up by urgency when writing about the City nowadays.

My job was made easier by the friendliness of many of the people
who work there. Although the newspapers were busy with crash
stories and Guinness revelations, the City was still open enough to
discuss things. I'd like to thank those whose quotations litter the
book and whose opinions gave me something to work with.

Unfortunately I can't. Virtually everyone I interviewed only
agreed to talk on condition that their names didn't appear. It's easy
to see why: by the end of 1987, the bull market had collapsed and
the competition of the deregulated market was starting to hurt.
These days anything can lose you your job in the City, and the
least offensive remarks about your employers or co-professionals, if
attributed, can put the skids under you.

This has given me two problems. The first is that I can't thank
anyone by name in this preface – although I hope they'll accept a
general, unnamed thanks. The second is that, while writing the book,
I found myself stuck for a way to use my interview material without
endlessly reiterating, 'a banker said' or 'according to an anonymous
stockbroker' or 'in the words of a Lloyd's underwriter who wishes
to be nameless'. Wisely or not, I decided to generate a group of
fictitious, composite characters, who could speak the lines of the
people I interviewed, and relieve the book of an unwelcome layer of
reticence. Lucky Paul, Webb, The Ace Merchant Banker, Nick, Keith
and The American are creations. Everything about them is true-to-
life, in that they say nothing that wasn't said to me, and that they
have and do nothing that I didn't observe in my researches. They
do, of course, make remarks and possess characteristics that are
drawn from many different sources, but I hope that Lucky Paul, or

Webb, or the Ace Merchant Banker are internally consistent despite their multiple parentages.

Some people may be critical of the period I have chosen, broadly between October 1986 and October 1987. There are other cardinal moments in the City's history, other ways to carve up the monumental complexity of the place; but, as my publisher and I agreed when we met for the first time on Monday 19 October 1987, this one was too good to miss.

C.J.

1

OCTOBER 1986: THE STAMPEDE

The City of London is a little place; it occupies an area of about one and a half by one and a half miles. Some people don't even know what the 'City of London' means. They think that it's like central London, or the West End, or Greater London, or something to do with the Tower of London.

But the City of London, the financial City, is important: without it Britain would be immeasurably poorer. Whenever some pop-eyed commentator appears on TV to explain how Britain's trade figures have gone into the red for another month running, he also, inevitably, points out that 'invisibles' have stopped the trade figures from being even worse. Invisibles are invisible overseas earnings, abstractions which are worth more than cars or ships or telephone exchanges. A large part of the invisibles is the product of the City's ingenuity and industry. The City's contribution by way of banking, insurance and financial services for 1987 was around £10bn. The gross income from the provision of financial services in 1986 was £51bn. This is nearly a sixth of Britain's total gross domestic product. The City also employs around 500,000 people, and makes work for tens of thousands of others in the West End, in the suburbs and in the provinces. The City is everywhere. It affects the running of the company you work for. It affects your property insurance, your pension, your savings, your life insurance, the funding of your local council, the relative morbidity of British industry and the shape of the economy. It affects the money you get for your travellers' cheques when you flop out of the plane in Malaga, and the likelihood of your having a job when you get back from Malaga two weeks later.

The City spent the first half of the 1980s, reinventing itself. It had to prepare for a new age, for the 1990s and further, if it was going to sustain the invisibles. But, as is the way with revolutions, the City's revolution, while achieving the broad goals it set out for

1

itself, also started to deviate. It attracted outside interest; things started to happen that weren't in the plan. The revolution plunged on in the direction it had chosen, but all the time, unwelcome, aberrant things kept piling up in the rush forwards. And some of the things the revolution was trying to get away from kept reappearing, like old promises.

It was a revolution which was always, slightly, out of control.

WAITING FOR BIG BANG

On Friday 24 October 1986, the London Stock Exchange closed in a state of mild apprehension. The Financial Times – Stock Exchange 100 Share Index (FOOTSIE as the City likes to garble it) stood at 1577.1, up 4.6 on the day. The brokers and market makers went home for the weekend, the richer ones off to the country. Some people might have been nervous but they didn't say so.

On Monday 27 October there was to be a thing called Big Bang. It was a great leap forward, a masterstroke, a cataclysm. The specialist magazines and the national newspapers were turning out fifteen-page special supplements on Big Bang; TV and radio had spent days nosing around, testing the views of the optimistic and the anxious, the diehards and the tyros. You couldn't turn on the television without finding a blanched securities expert hypothesizing on the new world which Monday was going to bring. No one had ever paid the City so much concentrated attention before.

So what was Big Bang? Crudely, it was the final excision of old restrictive practices which had featherbedded the City for years; the injection of fresh money, much of it from foreign sources, and the bringing in of technologically advanced ways of doing business. It was going to be the day on which the City of London, Britain's financial kingdom and the greatest single financial centre in Europe, would crawl over the parapet into the world of raw competition. It was the day for which a hundred agglomerations and combinations had been planning. It was the day on which the City would strip down to a pair of fighting shorts and stomp out into the ring to face, as it were, a thyroidal seven-foot Yankee and a Sumo wrestler weighing twenty stone and wearing his hair in a bun.

The weekend before, thirty-three market makers and 108 brokers had joined in a practice run for Big Bang. At 9 a.m. on the Saturday, they opened up the new computerized trading system, and had made around 12,000 fictional trades by lunchtime. The single most visible thing about Big Bang, was its technology. From Monday onwards, dealings in company shares and government debt were coming off the floor of the Stock Exchange, where they'd been since the eighteenth century, and were disappearing into one vast inter-linked computer network. Whereas before it had been man-to-man, now there was a *stratum* of hardware between you and your deal. If the hardware died, you died. You had to have it, because it was modern. All the same, for the first time in their professional lives the dealers and brokers found themselves trusting in another man's magic.

The Stock Exchange took notes, and decided that although there'd been difficulties in logging on and updating prices, the thing worked well enough. The market makers and brokers fooled around with the buttons. There was plenty of hilarity; and of course some of them decided after twenty minutes of thumb-twiddling that the system was too slow and too awkward. But what could *they* do?

It's taken a long time for the City to tunnel its way into our minds like this. Back in January 1975, the Stock Market crashed slowly and painfully to 146 on the Financial Times Thirty Share Index. That did make the headlines. Some people also might have noticed a sub-species of men known as 'financiers' who worked the City without apparently being a true part of it, men like Jim Slater and Harry Hyams who spent a lot of time being photographed by the newspapers before what were called their business empires imploded beneath them. Lord Poole of the merchant bankers Lazards felt comfortable enough in this atmosphere of careless tolerance to say that Lazards were a success because he lent money only to people who'd been at Eton.

Before that the City seems hardly to have existed outside the minds of the few who worked in it. The 1950s and 1960s are like a dream in which City types lived only to appear in cartoons in *Punch* magazine, or to be twitted on *The Frost Report* for being stuffy when everyone else was growing their hair. In the December 1963 issue of *Queen*, there was an article sneeringly entitled 'Are You Still Something If You're Something In The City?' The answer was, not really, when you could be a fashion photographer, or a hairdresser, or a Mod.

In fact the last time the City really seized the public's imagination (saving the Great Crash of 1929) was in the eighteenth century, at the time of the South Sea Bubble. There's even a chimeric familiarity about some of the contemporary reports. 'We are informed', a journalist wrote, 'that since the hurly-burly of stockjobbing, there has appeared in London 200 new coaches and chariots, besides as many more now on the stocks in the coach-makers' yards; above 4000 embroidered coats; about 3000 gold watches at the sides of whores and wives; and some few private acts of charity.' A few weeks later, ''Tis creditably reported that a little fellow, call'd Duke, a Change Alley porter, has got about £2000 by the Bubbles and is about to set up his chaise with a handsome equipage.'

Another paper pilloried a goldsmith who gambled so shrewdly on the stock market that he not only took to driving to work in Change Alley (still there, just off Cornhill) in a coach-and-six, but liked to parade around the neighbouring streets three or four times before actually stepping into his office. Robert Walpole struck the modern opposition stance in Parliament when he complained that the South Sea Company 'Countenanced the dangerous practice of stock-jobbing, and would divert the genius of the nation from trade and industry. It would hold out a dangerous lure to decoy the unwary to their ruin, by making them part with the earnings of their labour for a prospect of imaginary wealth.' The daunting cash purchases, the witless ostentation, the monster of speculation – where have we heard these before?

Only today's more cloacal wine bars are true inheritors of the City's eighteenth century past. But its physical location as the 'Great Maw of greed' is identical. The consumption and display of new wealth (grown magically from mere ideas) sound the same. But instead of the South Sea Bubble, we have the Great Bull Market and

Big Bang – metaphors which, in place of Georgian prettiness, suggest thunderous potency and the blast of creation.

THINGS HAD TO CHANGE

It took the City a couple of years of costive reinvention to get where it is now – a testimonial to its nerve. For most of the twentieth century, it had been letting go, like an alcoholic tackling his whisky earlier and earlier in the day, so that by the end of the 1970s, things had begun to happen which it couldn't contain or even understand. The Office of Fair Trading, for instance, was complaining about the Stock Exchange's restrictive practices. The matter had got as far as the Restrictive Practices Court, to force the Stock Exchange to jettison its habit of charging fixed minimum commissions on share deals. Elsewhere, investors had started to trade shares internationally after Exchange Controls disappeared in 1979, but instead of doing it through City firms (which hadn't the resources) they did it through foreign firms. It was even difficult for the broking firms to raise the money to operate with. The amount a single shareholder could own of a broking house had to go up in a series of wincing adjustments – first 10 per cent, then 29.9 per cent in 1982, and finally 100 per cent by March 1986 – before the Rowe & Pitmans and the James Capels and the Phillips & Drews could combine with any other really big financial institutions. Then at last they found they actually had enough capital to go to work in the modern world.

The technology was primitive too. Even though it was possible to trade shares over the phone (and unavoidable with international deals), the Stock Exchange still required the social participation of jobbers and brokers on the floor of the Stock Exchange. No matter how modern the new, 1970, Stock Exchange building looked, it still incorporated a traditional dealing room, full of jobbers' pitches built (as a concession to modern ways) of go-ahead beige plastic. And the brokers still had to go down to the floor and strike a deal face to face with a jobber, and the spirit of the eighteenth century, and *dictum meum pactum*, were all lovingly reaffirmed.

But Nicholas Goodison, Chairman of the Stock Exchange, and Cecil Parkinson, Secretary of State for Trade and Industry, made an arrangement. Parkinson stopped the Office of Fair Trading's action, while Goodison wrestled the Stock Exchange into what some commentators were over-excitedly calling the twenty-first century. Banks and brokers joined up to present themselves to the investing world as toughly meritocratic outfits. Huge American houses like Citicorp and Shearson Lehman consumed little firms of English stockbrokers like Edward VIIth eating a lobster. The jobbers (who make markets in shares) vanished into a new world of football pitch-sized dealing rooms and ad. agency buildings. Sometimes the deals didn't work out. Toffs from a quiet, prosperous broking firm would move across the City into a tower block only to find that they couldn't even talk to, let alone work with, their monomaniac American colleagues. Experts in gilts and equities were forever marching out to more congenial homes. The bosses panicked when their methodically integrated dealing floors collapsed into marathons of aimless bickering. And at the end of this painful integration, the City burped up a lexicon of names like Akroyd Rowe & Pitman Mullens, Chase Laurie & Simon, Citicorp Scrimgeour Vickers, Barclays de Zoete Wedd — clanking, incredible names, names that sounded like Dutch army commands, names that gave you no clue as to what alien thing it was that was being named.

LUCKY PAUL GETS A JOB IN THE CITY

Let us imagine a typical City inhabitant from these days, a stock-broker, and let us call him *Lucky Paul*.

It is around this time that Lucky Paul, now 32, married and rich, traipses into the City for his first interview with a medium-sized firm of stockbrokers. He has no idea of what to expect. We may assume that there is no City tradition in his family. He is one of the new wave of virgins, bright boys who have chosen the City for the first time. He stares across the room at a gilt picture frame holding the first bond signed by the firm's founder. He is aware of a middle-aged man sitting next to him. The middle-aged man looks at him for a long time and then says, 'I like you . . .'

Lucky Paul, although stepping into his stockbroker's suit back in 1981, is really a creature of Big Bang and the mentality which went with it. He owes his new life to Big Bang.

Lucky Paul now works in the City as a stockbroker's analyst. He is number two in the electricals sector team. His hair is shot through with grey, and his eyes peer out from dark wells (the result of two consecutive years of 8.00 a.m. starts and 6.00 p.m. finishes). His basic salary is perhaps £75,000 a year. 'Initially,' he confesses, without a jot of irony in his voice, 'I found it hard to adjust to the job. Partly because of my socialist views, I suppose.'

These days, Lucky Paul's socialism lives an independent life in the part of his mind where he also keeps his cultural interests – which might be opera, cricket and watercolours – and his wife and children. It's a souvenir from university days, which end in 1981 – the low point in his life, when it dawns on him that there are no academic jobs if you're merely another middleweight arts graduate. He has no strategy in mind. He doesn't go into the City because he wants to be a stockbroker's analyst. It is a choice which somehow happens to him.

Indeed, at the time, it is really no more than an escape from anxiety. The national unemployment figures are making their own great leap forward from 1.5m to 3m in the space of two years. It generates a fear which gets into your bones whether you have no O levels or a degree. Third year undergraduates loiter in University Appointments Committees, steeling themselves for Accountancy or the Law. Lucky Paul similarly steels himself, even for teaching. But first he gets in touch with university friends who have gone to the City, asks questions, calls upon his pimply coevals from his public school, takes down names and addresses. Let's say he has a schoolfriend called Nick, now working as a Lloyd's underwriter. Nick gives him a three-course lunch made entirely from animal fat and sour wine, and a tour of the City. Paul's timing is unimprovable.

He writes twelve letters; to firms of stockbrokers, to merchant banks and to a couple of fund management companies. He ends up with four job offers. He chooses the old boy who said, 'I like you.'

While the rest of the country is rioting, the City hungrily consumes hundreds of real Lucky Pauls. It is now that the brochures from Kleinwort Benson, S. G. Warburg, Greenwell's and the rest at the Appointments Committee start to look less like messages from another world and more like serious propositions. Sensitive arts graduates who might have gone into publishing or education are becoming bond dealers and corporate financiers. Their mood is cheerlessly matter-of-fact. The City virgins gather in bigger and bigger numbers.

Paul starts off making no more, perhaps, then £4000 a year. As he likes to remind people, 'I had no real value, economically speaking,' he stretches expensively. A well-shirted wrist goes up here; a hand-made shoe points down there. A crescent of pale stomach appears behind his silk tie, streaked with gravy. 'I was learning, not contributing. It was their investment in me.'

But Paul's firm is successful. The following happens: the money improves. The firm he is working for merges with another outfit, and they in turn become part of a financial conglomerate which now turns over a very great deal of money. Lucky Paul sits tight, improving his skills, adapting the craft of essay writing to the journeyman trade of reporting on television manufacturers. He is also personable, in a shuffling, pedantic way, and it does him no harm to have been at a boys' public school, no matter what the firm's graduate prospectus claims. Even though he still has trouble reading a balance sheet, and some of the grosser mathematics have been known to explode in his face, no one thinks any the less of him for it.

And now, the rewards. Lucky Paul is neither ferrety meritocrat nor jaundiced toff, but a middle-class graduate with only a few serious affections and no desire to be anything other than usefully busy. On this modest basis, he makes over £1000 a week, drives a large German saloon, has taken out a mortgage on a four-storey house, and is looking for a holiday home in the country. He supposes that it's an irresponsible job. If he makes a mistake, it's no great deal ... If he makes a lot of mistakes, it is, 'But no one's going to fire me ...'

Lucky Paul's entrenched near enough the top of his team to know that the juniors will leave first if anything goes wrong. 'We're committed to continuing as a major player in the equities market,' he says, his voice getting deeper and more confident as the company song finds its way into his mouth. 'We're confident that our size and expertise will enable us to continue that way. I don't have to worry about the firm not being here in the morning.'

Does nothing bother Lucky Paul? Not the competition? Not the low esteem in which the rest of the country holds the City?

There are times when he's struck by the poverty of his working conditions. Unlike the dealers' floor below, his bit of office doesn't cost £5000 a square foot to rent and equip. All he gets is a cubicle made of glass and plywood into which goes a slag of company reports, statistical tables, books, magazines, PR handouts, shreds of the *Financial Times*, notepads, a dictionary, another analyst and Lucky Paul himself. He is separated from the rest of his labouring colleagues by nothing more than an inch and a half of compacted chipboard. Making over £1000 a week (he thinks to himself) and I'm working in a chipboard hutch!

And the line of analysts' cubicles stretches the full length of the room: buildings analysts, leisure analysts, oil analysts, good and mediocre analysts, bores, comedians, Lucky Paul, all in an unbroken chain of intellection.

If he's had an especially heavy lunch, he might decide 'I've had enough for today'. Lucky Paul takes a walk, does some shopping, has a swim. He feels unapologetic about the fact that he doesn't have to stay at the desk all day while others do. And when he loosens his shambling reserve, Lucky Paul contradicts the two City stereotypes which most of us casually carry around with us. He neither pours champagne down his throat in rowdy wine bars, nor bottles and bottles of claret in all-male restaurants and dining rooms. What he does is to drink a couple of glasses of wine or a pint of beer; if he's not with anyone he may yield to a Perrier. He only gets drunk (and then, quite decorously) four, maybe five times a year.

It's hard not to think that things have turned out very nicely for Lucky Paul, the archetypal stockbroker's analyst. He may have to be in the office by eight in the morning, but at least he doesn't have to stay until two the next morning, like the lawyers and the bankers when they're fighting to conclude a deal. He may have to work in a hutch, but it's not as bad as working in front of a TV screen, like his colleague, whom we shall call Webb. (Webb can be a broker working on the private client side. Webb the private client guy is older than Paul. He is also unglamorous and cynical.) Lucky Paul may be sallow, but everyone who works in an office is sallow. And the work is neither significantly repetitive nor dehumanizing. He can listen to Mozart in his car all the way from London to the country and back again and feel nothing but self-approval. Let the others become housemasters in damp prep schools! Why feel uneasy about wealth?

Share prices are rising as Paul eases himself into the job. The crash of the early 1970s has joined England's World Cup win of 1966, the coronation of 1953, the general strike of 1926, as mere history. In 1980, shares gain 25 per cent in one year. By 1982, despite Brixton and Toxteth, despite 3m unemployed, despite the fact that the total number of bankruptcies is increasing by 1100 a year, the FT 30 Share Index goes through 600 for the first time. The Wall Street bull market officially starts on 13 August 1982 (one investment fund, run by US brokers Merrill Lynch, will grow by 486 per cent within five years). By 1984, the government is selling off nationalized industries like Jaguar and British Telecom at a rate of three or four a year. Rothschilds, Kleinworts, Cazenoves, Schroders, just about anybody, are all making money.

The *Annus Mirabilis* inaugurated by the Big Bang is to be Lucky Paul's year. He finds himself in this implausible City, making enough money to keep his vast house and live a rich, civilized life. Never before has he had so much to spend, enjoyed earning so much. The money seems to come out of thin air.

KLONDIKE

While London managed to lose 90,000 manufacturing jobs between 1981 and 1984, it generated more than 45,000 jobs in the financial sector. The urge to be big, to employ a lot of people, was the same urge which compelled City firms to buy £100m of Computer equipment, to own new premises with an *atrium* and a jungle of fig trees growing in it, to pitch for every possible sort of business transacted in the City. It was an urge compounded of the two great forces which endlessly roam the place – greed and fear. Fear (if we don't balloon out like *they're* ballooning out, *they'll* eat *us*); and Greed (provided *they* don't eat *us*, we can make very big money because we will be global, and we will deal with the big customers, the customers who are bigger than nations).

It was also becoming clear that youths straight out of college, were naming salaries for themselves that their parents were only just ready to earn. Some American and Japanese banks actually tempted the young undergraduate to join them by offering a £2000 cash bonus. It was simple supply and demand. We need a lot of people, the City firms agreed. We all need the same people, because we are all going to replicate the same functions in minutely different ways. And we have more money than anyone else in the country. So thousands of youths were invited to a party.

They came from Oxford and Cambridge, inevitably; they came from Warwick University (strong maths faculty) and Sheffield (good on Japanese); in 1985, incredibly, Sussex University (remember student protest? Remember 'Out Demons Out'?) supplied two stockbrokers, and a banker for Rothschilds.

They gobbled up the literature in the Appointments Committees more enthusiastically than they ever had *Beowulf* or *The Concept of Mind*. When they took out the colour brochures from Salomon Brothers International, they were rewarded with visions of a parallel world where their *doppelgängers* (now eerily prinked and shaven) crinkled the corners of their eyes at some International Problem, or shook the hands of wild Paraguayan Finance Ministers in brown boardrooms. Jackie, Clyde, Olga and Keith posed, casual but alert, around Salomon Brothers' training documents. Mark, 'who joined the firm in 1984, is shown here with clients at the closing of a transaction . . .' There he was! What? No more than twenty-five years old, and already 'closing transactions' and wielding a heavy golden pen over a slab of documents, like Geoffrey Keane in *The Power Game* reruns.

Over at Morgan Grenfell, a photograph of a brick-chinned hero was explaining, 'You can expect to work hard, learn fast and travel far (from Toyko to Yemen to Morocco and back this year for me) but never be so foolhardy as to attempt to predict where you'll be in a year, next month, or even tomorrow . . .'

Sometimes, there was too much cultural ground to cover. The blandishments from the Orion Royal Bank lived in a textbook that looked like an astrologer's almanac. Lists of Public Bond Issues and Fixed and Floating Rate Certificates of Deposit were intercalated between copperplate engravings of the design and building of St Paul's Cathedral. Was there a pattern? Were you meant to spot the mathematical harmonies between circle, square and Floating Rate Certificates of Deposit? On page 48, there was an essay entitled 'Resurgam'. It began: 'Twelve years had passed since Wren first became involved with St Paul's . . .' It was answered on page 49 by 'Investment Management': 'In December 1985 Orion Royal established a separate wholly owned subsidiary, Orion Royal Bank Asset Management . . .' What was the connection? What covert science was being hinted at? Would they ask you about it in the interview?

At least Kleinwort Benson had a brochure you could understand. It bore a colour photograph of fourteen pamphlets arranged in a tidy semicircle with the caption, 'These leaflets describe the attractions of the various Barrington funds.' It didn't matter who Barrington was, provided there was no 'Resurgam'. A colour close-up of a pile of Lockwoods tinned fruit also made you feel that these people had homelier things on their minds than the Orion Royal Bank, although a tyro with a telephone was quoted as saying 'Why KB? They are an aggressive organization who are looking to expand into new areas and offer excellent career prospects for graduates', to reassure you that they weren't homely to the point of comfiness.

And when Warburgs said that investment bankers could start off on a salary of £13,500 'plus normal banking benefits', you would have to have been utterly without character, to turn them down. So the bright ones left university at twenty-one and signed up. According to a Professor Goodhart of the London School of Economics, no less than 60,000 financial jobs were created out of the ether between 1985 and 1987.

The great tide of virgins coming into the City was impressive, purely as an exercise in new priorities; as the sign of a rejuvenated capitalism. But the most impressive thing about Big Bang to look at, was the hardware – the computers and all the material that framed them.

Before Big Bang, a lot of people had kept abreast of share price movements with a system called TOPIC. This was a videotext information service organized by the Stock Exchange. Like the domestic ORACLE or PRESTEL, this gave you pages of computerized words and numbers, but had no way of letting you feed back into the network. Salesmen and analysts, and anyone else who wanted to buy the service, could have a little TV built into their desks, with a typewriter keyboard in front of them, and keep up to date.

But this wasn't enough. It had to be interactive. There had to be a system which allowed users to feed in their own numbers and words. The new market makers after the Big Bang would have to be able to put up their own prices on the screen network (say, for shares in GEC or News International or Amstrad) and some sign of who it was who was offering GEC at 180p or News International at 250p. So the Stock Exchange invented SEAQ, the Stock Exchange Automated Quotation system, an interactive network riding on the back of TOPIC, but offering subscribers the chance to make a market.

They based it on the New York equivalent, the chunkily acronymed NASDAQ. They took NASDAQ and built on half as much computing capacity again. It meant wiring in over 8000 TOPIC computer terminals to the new scheme while leaving room for another 2000 subscribers to emerge over the next twelve months. SEAQ itself brought in thirty-two interlinked computers, housed in two separate buildings, which were then hooked up externally to another 200-plus computers in the offices of the interested parties. All the big firms and all the firms who wanted the other firms to recognize that they weren't exactly small, spent an estimated £4bn on mainframes, terminals, wiring and office furniture.

It looked terrific. Admittedly, it meant that the Stock Exchange floor was put out of business, and the Stock Exchange floor had a lot of things going for it as a single image of the working stock market – yobs and toffs scrumming around in a souk of TV sets, noticeboards and shreds of paper.

That particular vision of anarchy was going to die on 27 October. In its stead, we were given something which seemed both familiar and bizarre, a fusion of Churchill's bunker and a branch of Rumbelows. Now, there were to be things called dealing rooms. Every firm had one, and each one replicated the floor of the Stock Exchange inside a different building. They had low ceilings like cellars (even though they were on anything from the second to the tenth floor) and were lined with huge desks sub-divided into work stations. Each work station had not one, but three or four TV screens and maybe three diversely shaped keyboards. Whereas the old Stock Exchange floor made a pattern of reiterated hexagons, these were all lines and perpendiculars. While the old Stock Exchange had the dynamics of an obsessives' drinks party, the new dealing rooms were more like factories, or the insides of a great workshop. While the old Stock Exchange had the amoebic to-and-froing of the crowd, the new rooms caught a tension between the ordered ranks of the machinery and sheer human restlessness.

Dealers were now fidgeting, squirming and clutching themselves behind their four foot by four foot workstations. They tore off their jackets. They slumped against the hardware. They found a common posture in the same way that flamingoes will stand on one leg, or apes hang one-armed from a tree. They leant back in their chairs, pressed the phone confidentially to their chins with one hand, and sent the other hand back round to the nape of the neck, where it frayed the collar, smoothed the hairs, rummaged around on the scalp, did all the fidgeting for the rest of the body. Above all, dealers showed the world their armpits.

It was a new age. There was to be no more fuddy-duddy personal contact, only phone calls, and numbers punched into SEAQ and TOPIC. It was startling not just because the City – of all the country's snotty, hidebound institutions – had managed to transform itself; but because of the awful size of the transformation.

In just a few years, the City had gone mad for computers. It was not possible to be in the City without millions of pounds' worth of technology. The drawback was that no one who'd been in the City for more than three years could understand computers in any way. They felt admiration for them as gadgets, tempered with a visceral hatred of them as hard tokens of the modern world. So the City found itself hiring computer folk, like immigrant labourers, to work the problem out. Another character enters, here — Keith, the Computer Demon. Keith has been working for a little software company in London, when one of the new conglomerates buys him. Keith the Computer Demon, palefaced and nervous, has his reservations about the job.

They take him on, despite his expertise, much like any back office boy, any airheaded secretary: no better than the people whose job it is to unpin share transfers. 'I used to run the gauntlet when I arrived in the mornings. We're rather timid, introverted types by temperament not like the dealers at all.' You know what he means about 'the dealers' — sweltering, sumpy, not remotely impressed by the summation of technology and human cleverness with which they deal.

Because of this, the basic fascinations of Keith's work (managing huge cataracts of information in the quickest, most efficient and visually useful way) and the money he is paid are always tainted by the reactions he gets from his end users. 'When something goes wrong, they shout at you ... otherwise they just ignore you. Some people will only pick up the phone to swear at me. Dealers,' Keith mutters savagely, 'are very *brusque* and *rude* people, who only want *answers*, never anything else, just *answers*.'

Keith's agony comes from knowing that a dealer can have as little as thirty seconds in which to make the best trade, and if he hits the wrong button, or the right button which does the wrong thing, then the dealer is faced with a savage internal debate — how much to blame himself, how much to blame the machine, how much to blame the person responsible for the machine. This makes his rage at the lost deal even worse. Keith the Computer Demon knows it, but it still hurts when an 'ape' (without even a university degree) starts shrieking abuse down the phone into Keith's other world.

And yet Demon Keith is philosophical (and idealistic) enough to say that the whole grind is worth it when they find out that a rival's glittering, fresh-from-the-maker's, system is as much as forty seconds slower in operation than Keith's handtooled software. Now his computer-friendly boss is spending something like £23,000 on each new dealer's desk. 'The system I'm working on,' he insists, 'is going to have *absolutely the latest graphics.'*

Then, asks Webb, the man who knows it all, what's the final benefit from all this knowledge and power? Is it really to be found in a 14 inch TV screen bearing the SEAQ display of illuminated prices (blue for going up, hysterical red for going down), glowing away in front of a dealer? It is not. Old-school jobbers, used to loafing about their plastic booths, don't approve of it. It's all chips, isn't it? You can't do business with a chip. Things'd be what? *Hundred* times better if it was still face-to-face. Is it an electronic heaven? No. It is a television set that hurts your eyes.

Or is the final reduction of all this hard work and technical brilliance really found in a spell-checking programme for share analysts, which isn't programmed for brand names? 'Our spell-checker was *crap,'* a broker complained to Keith, the Computer Demon. 'Every time I typed in "Pepsi", it came back, "Papacy"?'

THE EMBARRASSMENT OF THE PAST AND THE FEAR OF FOREIGNERS

The very name Big Bang is ripely symbolic. It harkens back to an act of universal creation; but it also suggests diffuseness, chaos, violent, random activity. It hopes for a new creative order but fears a universal disintegration. Everyone fell on it without hesitation.

While the virgins – and Lucky Paul and Keith the Computer Demon – were swarming into the City, those who were already there were taking the chance to avenge themselves. The Big Bang, and the energy it summoned up, were directed at the past as well as the future. The new age was going to annihilate all the carpings and sneering that the rest of the world loved to rain down on the City. It was the City's chance to conquer its own embarrassing history.

What had the critics been saying? Well, among other things, they said that for years, the Stock Exchange had been underperforming as a source of overseas earnings; that the indigenous merchant banks were dwarfish and indolent in comparison with those of the foreigners; that Lloyd's, the insurance market, was making money but was profoundly corrupt; that 95 per cent of the overseas investments made by UK pension funds had to be handled by overseas firms because the City brokers were too small and unworldly to do so. Then there was the tale of the Eurobond Market, for instance. This grew, from 1960 onwards, into the largest bond market in the world. Eurobonds were invented by Siegmund Warburg (the German Jewish emigré who founded Warburgs and who by brilliance and force of character got on terms with the City) and are consequently thought of as a British financial invention. The City of London is the world market place for these things. But by 1986, not one of the fifteen leading Eurobond houses was owned by a British institution. The Americans, the Swiss, the Japanese, the Germans, the French, had all cornered the Eurobond market. Credit Suisse First Boston alone were doing an estimated $20bn of business. The British Banks were nowhere because, when the market was developing, they were too small or nervous or calcified to get a decent share.

Even as late as the 1980s there was a story that Robert Maxwell had given a $300m portfolio to the American firm Goldman Sachs to sell, precisely because of their modern approach to business. While the British brokers were only willing to take small unfrightening chunks of the portfolio onto their books at a time, Goldman Sachs said, okay, give us the whole $300m, the whole bundle. We'll take the risk that we won't be able to sell it (and consequently screw up our finances), but we'll also take the profit if we do. This assessment of risk for profit looked like collective delinquency to the British firms. But Goldman Sachs made the profit, and the British firms just looked peeved.

That's the sort of thing no one would be able to say about the City, ever again – even though the place is now wide open to foreigners. In fact, the City has the most relaxed and approachable attitude to foreign institutions of any of the major world financial centres. It has to, in order to keep its global usefulness. As a consequence, they're here in the most extraordinary numbers.

There are various ways of being foreign. You can be a hybrid, both alien and domestic, like a firm of British brokers called Capel-Cure Myers, now owned by the Australia and New Zealand Bank; or in with the Americans, like Shearson Lehman, now owners of the British house, L. Messel. An outfit like James Capel, very British, is owned by the Hong Kong and Shanghai Bank, utterly Chinese, but which in turn, is populated by belligerent Scots expats. Nowadays, some seventy-five of the Stock Exchange's member firms are owned by foreign houses.

Even Lloyd's, the last piece of the City to modernize, the most frankly Dickensian institution in the place, is partly owned by Americans, like Marsh McLennan (who bought up a British firm of insurance brokers called Bowring's) and Alexander & Alexander (who consumed Alexander Howden).

Or you can be simply foreign, like Morgan Guaranty, or Nomura. There's nothing fundamentally strange in the idea of foreignness. The City's already clogged with firms from Iran, Kuwait, Belgium, Brazil, Togo, Gabon, parts of Latin America which don't even have economies, parts of Africa where the philosophy of money has disintegrated back into barter, anywhere you care to name ... At the last count, there were 572 foreign financial institutions, based in and around the City. You get the same feeling walking down Gresham Street as you do from rubbernecking at a Heathrow flight departures board.

But they are in among the natives, these days; whether on their own account, like the big Japanese and American houses, or inmixed so that the column of Anglo-Saxon names on the firm's writing paper abruptly skids into French-Swiss or Nowhere City, Iowa. Twenty-five years back (with the exception of the great Siegmund Warburg), the chances were that if you were in the City, you'd been shunted up from a British cradle, through prep school, through a senior boys' public school, maybe the army, maybe Oxford or Cambridge, and finally into the City, where you were like a Crufts exhibit, displaying your historically authentic points; or even a kind of British Samurai.

But now, take a trawl through Becket's Directory of the City of London. On the one hand, we find The Hon. Thomas Jaster

18

Manners, Deputy Chairman of Lazards (Educ. Eton); on the other, Frank E. Horack III, M.D., Corporate Finance, Chase Investment Bank Ltd., born Bloomington, Indiana; recreations: motor racing and jazz. On the one hand, John Chippendale Lindley (Chips) Keswick, Chairman of Hambros Bank, born Shanghai, educ. Eton; on the other, Tsukasa Tanaka, Associate M.D. of Nomura International Ltd.; Jean Jacques Rousseau (yes, really), born Youngston, Ohio, and one-time Chief Operating Officer, Merrill Lynch Europe Middle East Ltd.; Daiwa Bank's General Manager, Kazutaka Ishii.

These people are rich as well as foreign. They are so rich that they inhabit the same kind of stupefying, theoretical world as particle physics or the mapping of the galaxy. Now, that *is* worrying. The world is given over more and more to corporate power. Countries shrink to the level of companies, as companies attain the majesty of countries. Britain is now Great Britain Plc, a holding company with interests in oil, aerospace, telecommunications, car manufacture and agriculture. In this world of small horizons and gargantuan corporate philosophies, you need muscle. You need money.

There are a number of ways of describing the financial muscle of a given institution. *Euromoney* magazine riskily had a stab at it by taking the market values of the world's biggest firms and assembling them in what it called the 'Banking Power Ratings For 1987'.

The Japanese Sumitomo Bank came out top. But the figure that comes attached to the Sumitomo Bank makes no sense in the ordinary world. It only starts to have meaning when compared with things of a similar size. The Sumitomo Bank was given a market value of $35.36bn. This would be enough to buy every single person in the United Kingdom, a video recorder, or a copy of the *Guardian* every day for five years. How much *is* that, exactly? To put it another way, it makes the Sumitomo Bank about $3bn bigger than General Electric, the supercolossal US engineering and technology company. In fact, Japan's Nomura Securities, who were placed second, could also trounce General Electric, with a capitalization of $33.9bn. Both of them are more than twice as large as our own British Telecom, rated on the same system. But the Americans are *stupidly* big. Aren't they? What's surprising is that going on *Euromoney*'s evaluation, the only US concern to make it into the top

19

twenty-five is American Express – which it then dismisses as being more an insurance company than a bank. The first non-Japanese institution coming in at tenth place is the Union Bank of Switzerland, with £15bn. The first British bank is in the number thirty slot which goes to the National Westminster Bank.

But *Euromoney* really saves its bile for the Rothschilds, the Kleinwort Bensons, the Hambros. The largest merchant bank in the UK was Morgan Grenfell with a market capitalization (at the time of the survey) of $804m. This doesn't even put it in the top hundred. It makes it no less than 42 times smaller than Nomura Securities. Even if you added up the market capitalizations of Morgan Grenfell, Kleinwort Benson, Warburgs, Hill Samuel, Hambros *and* Schroders, they would only just scrape into the top forty, and still be smaller than the Hong Kong and Shanghai Banking Corporation.

These are the kind of statistics which cause some City people to lose sleep. Lucky Paul, working away in the shade afforded by his very large parent company, disdains fear. He says, 'If the City can underwrite the financing of the Channel Tunnel, I can't see us having a lot of problems in the immediate future,' and waves the issue away . . .

But what about a Schroders man? What does a house like Schroders do? Webb, who has some private knowledge of Schroders, also has a little homily on the subject.

'Schroders', he says, 'are the last word in blue-blood merchant bankers. You really have to be a Schroders man to get on there. There's probably a Schroders prep school by now, getting them young enough . . . And while they're *very* good at maintaining their contacts, particularly with politicians, they're not *adapting* to the modern world. I mean, Schroders will produce a beautifully written memorandum, not a split infinitive in sight, but who *needs* beautifully written memoranda? They turned out a fantastic document on takeovers, 70 pages of it, a classic in its way, and distributed it, but who wants to read 70 pages? No one's got the time for 70 pages.' Webb is a hard man to please. For our purposes, he has a doubtful marriage, has turned forty, is not a star. Lucky Paul thinks that *he* has stardom ahead of him. Webb knows that his job is useful, but not the kind of thing that gets you quoted in the papers. So he brightens for a moment, says, 'I have absolutely no doubt that Schroders will be *eaten up* in the next few years. Maybe by a Japanese house.'

If you're very big (the City tells itself), you can wade through the mutilations of a ten-year business war, and get to the lucrative peace on the other side. And if you're very small and perfect then you can scavenge a living that way. If you're neither one nor the other, then you will be eaten up straight away, or your forces will slowly desert you, and then you'll be eaten up. Something will happen to you, that's certain. The trusty old immobility of the City has gone. The probability is, that what happens will be unpleasant. (It's already unpleasant, the City old boy thinks to himself. The City's lousy with technology; lousy with socially unsmart people; lousy with youth; lousy with competition; lousy with fear; lousy with foreigners.)

Big Bang is hardly a formal embrace of the future. It's a collision of terror, lethargy, greed – and it has granted an insight, an intuition to those who work there, of a world without the City. It has also led those involved to do some inexplicable things. One of the most inexplicable, and yet the most characteristic of the City's actions, was its posturing at the start of the new gilts market. It was the City, in its way, refuting the Eurobond calumny, and the mockery that went with it. It's like the £4bn investment in computerized dealing rooms. Once, says the City, we were incapable of action; now, we're capable of not just acting but going quite crazy.

The most significant thing about the market for British government debt, the gilts market, seems to be that you need a lot of money to break even. It costs a lot to finance, and only if there are a few players involved as primary dealers do these players stand a chance of getting rich. As Big Bang approached, the gilts market was opened up to a raft of new participants, many of whom thought that the gilts market would be a good thing to be in, while others thought they might as well stay out. Famous banks like Rothschilds, Schroders and Hambros didn't bother. Other famous banks, such as Barclays, Morgan Grenfell and Chase Manhattan did. Most commentators reckon the market can support about five or six players. Twenty-nine applicants lined up before the start. America's government bond market is ten times bigger than the UK one, but there are only forty primary dealers involved. This didn't trouble the City contenders. They had sneers and insults to deal with. Most of the firms involved were British; the Americans (who love to have a piece of the action, whatever it costs) were second in number; the odd Swiss and Hong Kong firm made up the rest.

Now, what sort of businessmen pile in so promiscuously with the competition for such chimeric rewards? What sort of sober financial institutions take a one-in-five gamble with the shareholders' money for no other reason than a yearning to be seen to be doing something? (Make a show of things! *They're* in the new gilts market! Why aren't *we*?) Like the ludicrous new buildings, the chaos of overstaffing, the frenzied equipment buying, it was more than a reaction to new business. It was the new, haunted by the stuffy inadequacy of the old.

Two of the twenty-nine firms lost their nerve even before the new market opened. The remaining twenty-seven soldiered on through 1987, and at the end of the year, twenty-four were left still playing, of whom only two had made any profits at all.

What's more, none of the firms which started off in 1986 was Japanese. The Japanese, with their unbelievable sums of investable money and their inhuman patience, will make ideal players in the gilts market, having no time for what is in effect a trial of manliness but only interesting themselves in things that they do well and profitably. At the end of 1987, Japan's two largest securities firms became gilts dealers, two years after all the rest. And that will be that for twenty British, American and Swiss firms.

AT LAST THE GREAT DAY

At 7.30 a.m. on Monday 27 October 1986, several thousand professional money makers, burning to try the new, fully-computerized system, keyed in their requests at the same time. If there was a moment at which Big Bang could be said to have happened, this was it. Lucky Paul's floor was busy with scabrous conversation. The new dealing rooms were twinkling with lights and polished TV screens. The men from the press and the television were waiting about. Weeks of coverage and guesswork and lists of players and essays about the new age were lined up, ready to fall on the Stock Exchange and the rest of the City if it didn't work.

They switched the system on. It broke down. The screens blacked out, no one could deal through SEAQ, and for a time, things had to go back onto the floor of the Stock Exchange. It was perfect. The outsiders could tie themselves in knots inventing squibs. Not with a bang but a whimper . . . Big Bang? More like big joke . . . As much popped balloon as Big Bang . . . How *could* £4bn's worth of technology ever be expected to work? This is EC2, not the Houston Space Centre. This is Britain, not Japan.

They tried again on Tuesday. Things worked until lunchtime, when the North American Prices service came onstream. Unfortunately, the Stock Exchange was also running a debugging procedure through the system at the same time; and some scallywag Stock Exchange official punched a RESET button which logged all the screens off, and then back on again, blank. Wednesday was better, but for the fact that Barclays de Zoete Wedd, Warburgs and Morgan Grenfell all discovered to their rage that they couldn't get any of their share prices into the system at the beginning of the day. There are three castes of stocks trade on the Stock Exchange: Alpha stocks, which are the blue-chip companies, and the most actively traded shares; Beta stocks which are essentially less so; and Gamma stocks, which, as you'd expect, are the most infrequently traded shares of the more negligible companies. By this time, dealers were so eager to believe that SEAQ would blow up again that they started rumours that the Gamma stocks would be taken of the screens entirely and put back on the now semi-desolate Stock Exchange floor to ease the network.

It was the old TOPIC system which was buckling at the knees. Before Big Bang, TOPIC had had to deal with perhaps 1m page requests per day. Once it was integrated with SEAQ, and Big Bang had happened, it had to manage no less than 3.8m page requests on one day. The NASDAQ system in New York, by way of comparison, carries more securities, but only has to deal with 500,000 page requests a day. The Stock Exchange found to its mingled horror and satisfaction that SEAQ could quote 2500 securities and generate 62,746 price quote changes in a single nine-hour period during week one of Big Bang. Nicholas Goodison appeared on TV from time to time, looking flushed and hectic, as if he'd spent the day up in a cheap hang-glider.

On Thursday, they decided to restrict user access to certain closed user systems, by changing the passwords involved. This was meant to take some of the pressure off, and keep SEAQ going. Then it was decided to cut out some of the lesser services altogether, to help resist the avalanche of demand, until the new hardware and software (due in eight months' time) appeared. And that embarrassed shrinkage of its ambitions more or less saw the Stock Exchange through to the end of the week, by which time only a third of business was being transacted on the old Stock Exchange floor. Within another week, the floor would be deserted. The network was still several percentage points off complete reliability. It meant that every fortieth screen transaction, or thereabouts, was likely to disappear into the wiring and never be seen again, but that was something you lived with. And if you were getting SEAQ to work most of the time, it actually seemed like a good idea. Of course, the outside world had made its Big Bang jokes by then, and was losing interest, except for the kind of morbid attentions you might pay to a gambler on a losing streak, or a British athlete, spreadeagled in front of the main stand, having tripped on his own shoes in the long jump.

But it worked. The City was wise to the new age. FOOTSIE closed briskly up 9.1 at 1586.2, on day one of Big Bang. By Friday evening, it stood at 1632.1, up 55 points on the week. The bars were stuffed with back-slapping know-alls and bumptious tyros. The *Annus Mirabilis* had begun.

Things were happening. There was a thrilling conflation of old and new: gadgets and traditions; middle classes sitting down next to lower middle classes; toffs rubbing up against meritocrats. And while the toffs were discovering the ways of the ferrety meritocrats, the meritocrats were learning about the City. They found themselves in a place unlike any other place they'd seen. In fact, they found the physical City, the buildings and streets, as strange as hell.

Other parts of London – Westminster, Soho, Hampstead – merge into their neighbours. They're just parts of London, like postal districts or pages in an *A to Z*. But the City tells you when you're entering and leaving it, not simply by the gradual massing of office blocks and imperial clearing banks, but by a bronze dragon, forty feet high, in the middle of the road where the Strand and Fleet Street join. That marks its western limit. The northern boundary, at the junction of the Gray's Inn Road and Holborn, has dragons too – two stone obelisks are topped by these silver monsters at Holborn Bars. Once you've seen the dragon, you find it everywhere, panting away on street names and doorways, bursting out into metal bas-reliefs and stone effigies. It brands the pavement you walk on and the gap of sky between the buildings. It even brands the City of London police, who grow a blackened wen on their helmets, bearing the dragon. You know the City, even as it detumesces into Stepney and Shoreditch, by the panting dragons, and the motto *Domine Dirige Nos* which beseechingly underlines them. The City is rubricked with beasts like devils, and prayers to God.

In fact, it's like a tiny country within a country. It's the Lichtenstein of Britain. The dragons and prayers to God denote a corporate county where the Lord Mayor, twenty-five Aldermen and around one hundred and fifty Common Councilmen run the Corporation of the City of London. There are two sheriffs, whose ancestors were portreeves of London and Middlesex. The City itself is carved up into twenty-six wards, and the wards have reekingly fusty titles like Cordwainer, Vintry, Portsoken. The very street names, Old Jewry, Saint Mary Axe, Change Alley, are like an American film producer's dream of Albion. The spot where Temple Bar now is, used to be the place where traitors' heads were spiked for public view, where Titus Oates was left in the pillory, where the Queen (on state occasions) has to ask permission of the Lord Mayor of London to pass through into the City.

There are still Livery Companies, to which important City types may belong. Twelve of them are 'Great'; the remaining sixty-two simply exist. The Worshipful Company of Fishmongers, number 4, is a Great Livery Company, and got a very early patent from Henry II in 1154. The Company's prime warden is lucky enough to be assisted by someone known as a 'Barge Master'. Living people, lawyers and bankers, stockbrokers and chartered accountants, they belong to these Livery Companies, or are members of the Honourable Artillery Company, the oldest military body in Britain. At Marble Arch and South Kensington, mere places in London, people have jobs and ordinary lives. In the City, a bank director in the Honourable Artillery Company may march through the streets with a fixed bayonet and flying colours.

More than this, the City of London actually embodies the idea of a city more thoroughly than anywhere else in the country. The most complete imagined city, the most city-like of all places, would be a mixture of Piranesi's engravings, Turner's Rome, Doré's *London*, Fritz Lang's *Metropolis*, and maybe Ridley Scott's *Blade Runner* – a place where the geometry of buildings and sky looms over a race of hyperactive midgets, sometimes humiliating them in enormous bleak squares and piazzas, sometimes burying them in gorges between the steel and masonry.

The City is much like this. There are some very tall buildings, like the Stock Exchange or the NatWest tower; even Kleinwort's stubborn block near the Monument. Blocks are what you'd expect in the ideal city. But the City isn't a patch on New York for sheer height. What the City (the perfect city) manages is to set over a century of mismatched architectural styles against one another, ordered but chaotic, like a vision of Piranesi, comprehensible but threatening.

Some buildings, like the NatWest's old National Provincial edifice in Bishopsgate, come from a financial-imperial age, in which Corinthian columns, pilasters, goddesses, the whole business of a

Graeco-Roman temple, are drafted into something which is half-way between a bank and a consulate. In the NatWest's case, their forefathers opted to improve as well as belittle the passers-by, with a series of bas-reliefs running along the uppermost part of the façade. At one end, rude artisans are compelled by a Britannia to do something more with their lives than sit naked in the British rain. By the other end, the artisans have, thanks to the goddess, put on construction helmets and crafted a Bessemer converter which they wield bravely over the street below.

Big and little versions of the financial-imperial style dot the City. The NatWest's is striking because of its copybook excesses. The Bank of England building is striking because of its size, its fortifications, its towering, pyramidal summit, apparently somewhere in the clouds where the Governor of the Bank of England (you imagine) sits in the highest room with an ingot of gold in his lap and a map of the colonies spread in front of him. The Bank and all buildings like it recall a time when the City financed the world, brought railways to America and diamond mines to South Africa; when its foreign investments were as much as those of all other countries put together.

Financial-imperial took a long time to die. Between the wars, it mutated into a fascist style which took the imperial proportions but threw away the goddesses and pilasters. Then, after the blitz, there emerged the concept of the building as machine — not in the Le Corbusier machine for living sense, just a machine. These are the things that line up along the London Wall and Paternoster Square — buildings which are like white goods or kitchen appliances; the 1950s and 1960s developments whose formal blankness is meant to betoken a kind of streamlined thought, a spare, clean devotion to function. The kind of people who come out of these buildings, they say to you, wear modern fibres, and get things done. These people, they say, are as efficient and reliable as an office franking machine.

Then the office blocks come to look more and more like pocket calculators, and the pocket calculators come to look more and more like office blocks. This is fitting, as the work involves more pure intellection, the computation of bigger and bigger numbers. And it gets to the point where Richard Rogers designs the new Lloyd's building and says to the world, this building really *is* a machine for thinking. Look, imagine that the bare steel girders and buttresses are the grids and circuit-boards and connectors with a few six-foot diameter steel wires coming out, that these unaccountable steel whorls are capacitors, and these little mobile things are, uh, micro-chips, only they're called insurance brokers and underwriters. It all fits. The fact that Lloyd's, of all the City's institutions (saving the Baltic Exchange) is the one spiritually closest to the nineteenth century, is not important. The statement is important. In fact, the building may even be the final word in social engineering. It may yet turn a Lloyd's underwriter, after five or six years of confinement, into a dynamo of pure thought.

Now, all these architectures fan out from the Bank, along Lea-denhall Street and Gresham Street and Moorgate, making canyons of dust and concrete for City hurricanes to blow down. As you stumble down one of these streets, the buildings move in and out and rise up and diminish. Dashwood House, fifteen storeys in deep pink, rises like a tombstone over a demented French Empire-style parade of shops in Liverpool Street. Buildings change their textures and shapes and colours, but all, in the best Piranesi madhouse style, are relentless. They stand high and impenetrable, while you scuttle about at ground level. And they compound your vertigo and throbbing inferiority in the street, by not having any doors. Rather, they have two sorts of doors, neither meant to let you in. They have triumphal doors, to announce the fact that the building you're entering (or just hurrying past) is not a building to be fooled around with, and you'd better take care, because there are powerful folk in here; or zany secret doors, sometimes giving onto the street, some-times hidden up an alley, but always locked and neglected, and used only for some baffling, obscure, quadrennial purpose.

Other parts of London are full of doors and windows. There are shops to browse in. There are restaurants and bars. There are houses, flats, people's front doors, and curtained rooms. In the City, the doors are infrequent and uninviting. The windows admit light, but tell the traveller outside nothing of the humanity inside. What shops and pubs there are are furtive. Some places actually prefer to hide underground; you have to go through ornamented cave entrances to get at them. The Underwriter (a pub near Lloyd's), The Throgmorton restaurant, the Gallipoli restaurant (complete with a stained-glass onion dome, lantern and blue-glaze tiles) are all subterranean. Do they do this to avoid building on expensive, overused City land? Or are there people who like it beneath the daylight world? What troglodytes live ten feet underground?

But the real *Metropolis* feeling gets you when you stand still. Everyone else hurries. They have to get from one office to another. They have to scoff up a sandwich and a cup of tea for lunch. They have to race to the train to get home. Best of all, on a winter's evening the office lights, still burning furiously away, cast an authentically stagey limelight on the crowds below as they head, magically in the same direction, for the evening trains. No one talks much; it's quite quiet. And after a day's staring at the TV screens or slumped over the paperwork in a modern office, the commuters look plausibly drugged. It's *Metropolis* all the way through to the odd lone figure who struggles against the sea of humanity, to go south while they head north; or to go east while they point west. Who is that tiny, fragile person? What does he know? All that's missing are Fritz Lang's little biplanes and monorails zipping between the highest floors of the skyscrapers. It's the perfect, imagined, nightmare city.

Into this city, this other country, comes the graduate, eager for his new job, or the toff, transported from the nineteenth century into a multinational garage of money, where the computers line up over the Temple of Mithras, and the National Provincial's Graeco-Roman consulate of finance confronts Standard Chartered's gargantuan microwave, and they may wonder what confection of history, science and adventurism they're working for.

2

NOVEMBER AND DECEMBER: PROFESSIONALISM

The great event had happened, and the City was henceforth part of a new age. It was a new city, in fact – a rejection of all criticism, an embodiment of the best of the new and the most fruitful of the old.

If the City were a person, it would probably be somewhere between George IV and Mr Pooter. It tries to restrain all kinds of improper desires, while giving way at the same time, to a zoo of impossible fantasies. It mixes up contradictions of professionalism and guesswork; sobriety and gambling; old and new; charlatanism and intellect; honesty and absolute venality. The Big Bang, like so much of what the City attempts these days, was a gesture of terrified hope. It was a confidence trick, in two senses: it dressed the City up as a vividly new technological metropolis for the benefit of the wider world; and it was also an attempt by the City to persuade itself that it had a future. But over and over again, in the wrack of impressions, you see the unregenerate obsessions of the old place crawling out through the cracks in the cement and anodized steel and plastic and glass.

But the professionalism of the City – that doesn't change. In fact, it's more ruthlessly hard-working and rigorous than it ever was. That's one product of everything that led up to Big Bang. The City is full of smart people. It's full of money and clever guys. That's what the City argues. Not everyone else, of course, accepts this point of view.

TALKING TO THE FINANCE KING

If you are a client of the big City institutions, if you are, say, a chemicals and paints producer; or a white goods manufacturer; or a construction company; or better still, if you are any of these things but big, big to the point of being multinational, bigger than countries themselves, then the City is, actually, quite a small place to you. Talk to a Finance King with a multinational company and he disdains a lot of what the City seems so pleased with. Maybe it's just his need to repudiate the drawling toffs. Maybe he ransacks his heart for some respect and honestly can't find any. Either way, he says if you work for a big multinational, *they* come bowing and scraping to *you*. 'If we didn't exist, the City could carry on trading among itself for a few more months and then . . .'

His view of life is quite different from the merchant bank tyro's moving-and-shaking philosophy, or the Olympian disdain of a broker's analyst (who believes himself to be a kind of Voltaire of free market capitalism). He thinks that the world moves because people make things for other people and sell them at a profit. Bankers, brokers, insurers, just make it easier (or occasionally harder) for the engine of the world to keep going. 'We have two main merchant banks, but we keep on . . . twenty-three? Twenty-four others?' This is novel. You might get the impression from the City that the rest of the world congratulated itself every time it mastered its social dread and got off the train at Bank station – that the story of Cazenoves', the grandee stockbrokers, clients only being allowed upstairs to the directors' rooms via the service lift was really a symbol for all relationships between the City and everyone not from the City.

But the Finance King says that he is sitting on the money, and he can shop around. He doesn't have to ask; they have to attract him. Some firms are better at one thing; some are better at others. 'They say, we'll offer you a total in-house financial service, but if you've got some money stuck in, say Malawi, they come back and say we'll sort it out, just give us a few days, and you know perfectly well they haven't the faintest idea how to get *anything* out of Malawi. So you go to someone who has.'

As he warms to his theme, the Finance King begins to sound even more wildly condescending than the City people are meant to. There's a conflict of philosophies beneath this. The Finance King believes the power of the world to be with him; the City believes the skill to use this power is with itself. The person who wins this muffled battle of identities is the one who acts as if he's won. The public school banker gazes down at the grammar school Finance King who revenges himself by trumping him. 'There *are* all these frightfully laid-back public school types, and they sit around and say, frankly I haven't the faintest idea about equities — the corporate finance director at a major merchant bank (ha!) actually said that — but they can do the job' (a dismissive gesture of sufferance, here) '... pretty well ...'

Not only that, but the Finance King, steadfast in his very large multinational company, actually feels more secure than his opposite numbers in their inexorable new world of City competition. It hasn't escaped *him* that the same laws of business which he deals with day-to-day are now bothering them. So the satisfaction he feels when he contemplates this great levelling of human ambition taints every word he speaks. The big firms survive, the little firms don't. His view is more fundamental than the City's own. He allows himself the multinationalist's luxury of seeing a world populated only by more multinationalists. 'Warburgs will survive, and so will BZW, and probably NatWest ... Barings will live on,' (Barings? They're not so big. Why Barings?) 'because they own the freehold to Bishopsgate ... but I don't know about ... *Cazenoves* ...' This is it: the monotone dismissal of Cazenoves, the snottiest brokers in the world, the people who stick their clients in the service lift, who are so proud that they spurn partnerships with ordinary banks to lift their capital base, who merely 'make provision' to ensure their commercial liquidity in all events. (What do they do? Sell a Holbein? Ask their titled friends?) A lot of people assume that Cazenoves will never go under, like the Royal Family or the BBC, because they're too grand not to survive. But the Finance King (like Webb, the cynic) loves to tinker with the thought of Cazenoves having to sell up their fruity, swagged mansion in Tokenhouse Yard and go to work for one of the high street clearing banks.

He even lets you know that he, personally, can afford to turn his back on the place. 'People have tried. Oh yes. I've been headhunted. The phone rings all the time. But you wouldn't get me to work in the City. It's a terrible place. The only thing that keeps these guys working in the City is the money. That's the only thing. I'm certain of it ... And if you said to one of these guys, you're getting £15,000 a year instead of £50,000, then they sure as hell wouldn't stick it.'

THE CITY IS PROFESSIONAL

That's the Finance King for you. The City, of course, looks on itself with more approval. There's too much written and said about the money that these City tyros are paid; the stupid cars they drive, and the habits they acquire. What the rest of the world forgets, says the City, is that we are real professionals now. It's not good enough to try and needle us by saying that stockbrokers are merely salesmen, bankers merely usurers. We do some clever things, things that you couldn't do.

Lucky Paul, for instance: although much of his work looks like the leavings from a plutocrat's table, it takes Lucky Paul time, effort and thought, to turn out his apophthegms: The yield is attractive and strong cash flow augurs well for a further reduction ... things are beginning to happen ... the recent US acquisition looks like a very good one ... buy if you think the market has stabilized ...

This all requires work. He has to visit the companies he specializes in, beadily inspect them in a tour round, and feast himself on the company's various PR material and business announcements. Then he has to ingratiate himself with the company head, to get an idea of what's going to happen to them, rather than what has happened.

It takes some learning. You start off as a junior analyst from Cambridge University, and you parrot the jargon which reveals your City smartness, and you learn about p/e ratios, yields, margins, you keep an eye on sector developments, and then you wind up in the Chairman's office, and he's fifty-two years old and he looks at you with a confused mixture of loathing and love, and *you* have to quiz *him* ... It is handy having a – well – *background* ... until you sit down to talk to a self-made man (the relentless Sir John Egan, the terrifying Alan Sugar) who thinks you're a complete *dunce*.

On top of which you have to glean prospects and new products and anything else that might give your investors the tip that'll put them ahead. Then you have to boil the thing down into a report that's short enough for your consumers (the fund managers, the salesmen, the private investors) to read, long enough to be complete, and shrewd-sounding enough to be authoritative. And you have to do it in a chipboard hutch with the brewery specialist next door, farting and gasping away like a rhino after a trip out to the Courage factory on the M4. Work? Yes, it's work. This is precisely what the City is all about – competitive service, brainpower.

Yet Lucky Paul sometimes wonders about the true value of his expertise; especially when he contemplates the real specialists, the kinked-gene men, the people who make their working City lives into a hommage to one act.

Most City people do a thing, and have only the sketchiest idea of what the others are up to. Lucky Paul's friend Nick at Lloyd's is an example. Webb would know what Paul does and vice-versa, but then they work in the same building, one feeding the other. But there are the Eurobond dealers, the foreign exchange dealers, the swaps experts, the corporate financiers, the futures marketeers, the options traders, the lawyers, the gilts analysts, the commodity brokers, the ship brokers, the computer operators, the chartists, the salesmen, all like so many fevered academics, all nourishing their little patch, all busily shaping and reshaping their skills.

Vertigo sets in when you try and cross from one discipline to another – especially from something approachable, like Paul's crushed essay writing, into, let's say, the options market. For an options marketeer, this kind of thing (from a specialist magazine supplement) is not just meaningful, but interesting: '... a quasi-put was invented. Chase Manhattan Bank offered $50m worth of Reverse Spins, for a 2 per cent three-year note linked to downside performance in the S & P 500 ... sharp-eyed hedgers will also create a synthetic long position when Reverse Spins are cheap, by buying the call and selling the put, or when Reverse Spins are rich, create a synthetic short by selling the Spins and buying the put . . .'

Now, anyone in a modern profession might be able to produce an equally mind-scrambling paragraph from the bottom of their briefcase, or from the piles of material littering their desk. Doctors, psychologists, vicars, engineers, lawyers, all turn language into a corkscrew for opening their special problems, rather than a way of making their problems explicit to anyone else.

Like any modern professional, the City person creates a mystery around what he does. Someone involved in the Euromarket will tell you, almost numb with the familiarity of it all, about the distinctions between debt convertibles, FRNs, droplock bonds, capped FRNs, and so on, while your mouth sags open and your head swims. Ask a swaps merchant exactly what the process is by which he rejigs a company's debt finance, and his answer makes no immediate sense. Is it a currency swap or an interest rate swap? How familiar are you with LIBOR? What do you know about Nomura's famous Heaven and Hell bond issue? Who are the Euro-yen reverse deal issuers? If you listen to the merchant banker explaining the structure of the famous Nomura Heaven and Hell swap, it might as well be an astrophysics conundrum for all the meaning it contains:

> . . . There were three separate swap counterparties . . . Coca-Cola . . . the Federal Home Loans Bank and the Toyo Bearing Company . . . there was a pivotal 10-year Heaven and Hell bond issue for the FHLB of ¥ 25,000,000,000 . . . the formula was $X = 5672.908 \times (1 + 1.143178 \times F - 154.1985)/154.1985 \times F \times 25,000,000,000/1,000,000$ . . . F equals the spot yen/dollar exchange rate at maturity . . . they created a synthetic Euro-yen issue swapped into dollars . . .

Merchant bankers like to work these things out on their tricky pocket calculators, and reminisce on deals they've made which had their own purity of line, their own perfect, consistent symmetry. Even if you escape from this and go to the Harrods Food Hall-style Baltic Exchange, even there (where it's what? Just matching up cargoes and carriers?), you still need some kind of secret understanding to disentangle the coded details about materials and vessels which brokers trade with one another.

Much of the City is comprehensible if you reach out and grasp the salient points as they drift past you. Market-making is buying cheap and selling dear. Analysis is thinking about things and writing reports. Insurance underwriting is about (as any Lloyd's man will tell you) the feeling you get in the seat of your trousers as to whether this, or this risk is a good one to cover. And while the City might be described as a huge agglomerate of expertise, it doesn't necessarily mean that all the experts are very clever — simply that they have highly-developed skills. That's where, to Lucky Paul's endless disappointment, it ceases to be a confederation of academics. There are thousands of simple City types who, faced with the abstractions of international finance, resort to happier ways of describing some of their features. The really clever people who invent financial instruments are called Rocket Scientists. If you want to issue a bond without any fancy conditions, you call it a Plain Vanilla Bond. The fancy conditions, when they do appear, are known as Bells and Whistles . . . the yearning for childhood . . . Dan Dare . . . ice cream . . . steam trains . . .

But the rest of the place is littered with seething thought and the generation of financial mazes. Intellectual processes generate more intellectual processes in answer to them. The solution to one financial problem creates two more problems for someone else to solve subsequently. An answer generates another question. The thing with the City's true expertise (says the City) is that it gets buried under a sludge of misplaced populist images and cracker-barrel conventions. City types drive fast, red cars! They never work! They drink until they're sick, every day of their lives! Stockbrokers are salesmen and bankers are usurers! Well, no, argues the City. We can be clever, as clever as Crick and Watson, as shrewd as Disraeli, as far-sighted as Karl Marx.

Right at the bottom of this, there are human needs arising from the thing calling itself the real world. You need money to live. After air, light and water, you need money. By organizing their cash requirements efficiently, companies become more profitable, expand — which is probably where *we* come in, right at ground level, in this great university of skills. When one country's fiscal policies turn to dust; when the Bretton Woods agreement on dollar convertibility disintegrates; when the Louvre Accord on exchange rates blows up; when the world decides that the US administration is running its economy like a bankrupt earldom — then the City experts lay into their calculators to invent new currency hedging devices, new ways of borrowing money internationally, new ways of keeping whatever profits you have, and which some administration is snuffing out for you.

The merchant banker (another invention: let's just call him the Ace Merchant Banker) with his pocket calculator and his vast salary, is in another league. He understands tremendous things. He has a kinked gene, and he loves the symmetry of a good swap, or the chance to move in on an interest rate differential which no one else has spotted. Now and then he simply makes $4m for the firm by noticing a discrepancy. 'All these clever people, all this incredible technology, and they still miss these arbitrage opportunities,' he says pityingly. The Ace Merchant Banker really is at home here, engineering tactics and creating for the bank's clients (the muttering Finance Kings) another breathing space, another chance to keep their money.

That's how the City likes to see itself — bustling with Rocket Scientists, pulsating with cleverness. It's the University of Finance. That's why it's so expensive. Forget about the brickhead toffs, the bond dealers from Canning Town who beat up Spanish wine waiters, forget about the shiftless portfolio managers and the lackadaisical analysts. Think about the Ace Merchant Banker. Think about the options expert who works so hard to find new ways of hedging your currency position, so that your company stays in profit and you keep your job. That, says the City, is why we're here.

HOW TO MAGIC MONEY

But the old City peeps through. The technocrats are still only part of the picture. You see, one of the principal beauties of working in the financial world is that you can generate money from thin air. In November 1986, right at the start of the *Annus Mirabilis*, Sir James Goldsmith showed everyone how a master of finance, a Prospero of money, could produce unimaginably large sums of money from something which was never anything more than an abstract proposition.

This was the Goodyear tyre company takeover bid. There was nothing to it: Sir James Goldsmith bought up 11.5 per cent of Goodyear, paying $42.20 a share. Using this as his starting point, he told the company that he was going to buy some more shares, and win the favours of the other shareholders, and carry on until he, not Goodyear, controlled Goodyear. This went on for a time and then died when the news came out that Washington had taken against raiders and contested takeovers. The Goodyear attempt was finished. Sir James Goldsmith allowed Goodyear to buy back his 11.5 per cent holding, and relieve him of his interest in the firm. The only difference was that they had to pay $49.50 a share, instead of $42.20. This meant a profit for Sir James Goldsmith of $93m. He called the takeover bid a failure, but it was hard to see how $93m in the bank was a failure in the same way that $93m *out* of the bank might have been called a failure.

This wasn't the first time Sir James Goldsmith had passed his hands magically over a corporate body, to conjure money. In 1983, he bought a conglomerate called Diamond International. He had a team of alchemists in New York, who broke up the muddy dross of Diamond International, and sold off its components. By the end of the exercise, Sir James Goldsmith had a net gain of 1.7m acres of trees, and a 200 per cent profit on his original outlay.

In 1984, he tried to acquire a paper company called St Regis, but was bought out. All the same, the sheer activity of acquiring shares with a view to a takeover had increased value of his holding from $100m to $150m when he sold off his holding. And again, in 1985, he consumed Crown Zellerbach (another paper company); got his alchemists to break it up, sell some bits, swap others; and found himself the owner of another 1.7m acres of trees, valued at $1.2bn, and for which he'd only paid $100m.

Goodyear was another piece of magic. It was as if Sir James

Goldsmith had moved into a world of metaphysical business. If I did *this*, he says, then *that* would happen. Sometimes it *does* happen, sometimes it *doesn't*, but the physical world below acts as if it will or is almost certain to. The very presence of Sir James Goldsmith causes share prices to move, whether he acts or not. Something will happen to you if it is known that Sir James Goldsmith is merely thinking about you.

Now, this conceptual arrangement between what you do and what you get is very attractive to the City. In fact, it lives to prove that there is no simple equation throughout the free market, between work and money, between action and reward; and that in the City you do not need a lot of one to get a lot of the other. The City may be a University of Finance, but it's also a place where the connection between what you do and what you earn is infinitely flexible. If you're an alchemist like Sir James Goldsmith, you can exploit this disjunction to make yourself rich. And this has always been the case. The City is there for some people to magic money out of circumstance, chance, timing.

Statistically, you were more likely to be over fifty than under thirty, if you were making £50,000 a year or more in the City, by the year of Big Bang. Nevertheless, enough people had such huge incomes, that any flat, mathematical assessment of salaries got hopelessly distorted. Barclays de Zoete Wedd were estimated to be spending about £100m a year on staff salaries, which, with a staff of 1800 meant that the average wage was £50,000 a year. A firm of brokers called Smith New Court (employees at the time of reckoning were 618) disclosed in its annual report, that the year's wages bill was £32.8m; in other words, more than £53,000 a head, including tea boys, secretaries, gofers and dealers.

In America, naturally, that kind of money really isn't money at all. A person called Michael David Weill, of Lazard Frères, claimed to hold down £75.75m per annum. Another American, Michael Milken, from merchant bankers Drexel Burnham Lambert (the man who invented the junk bond) took home around £40m between 1986 and 1987. Sir Ralph Halpern famously paid himself more than £1m for running Burton's, but from then on, the figures plunge into the sub-millions, banal money, the sort of money Michael David Weill would earn in a day. Somewhere, obliterated by this torrent of earning power, ordinary British folk were taking a year to get what they thought was a reasonable living, at around £15,000.

But the most startling fact was that in the second half of the 1980s, Britain's highest-paid man was to all intents and purposes, completely invisible.

Christopher Heath officially became Britain's highest-paid person when it emerged that he was earning £2,512,595 a year as managing director of Baring Securities (whose parents are Baring Brothers, the trad. merchant bankers). The news opened up a new area of mutual incomprehension. On the one hand, Christopher Heath, an ex-Ampleforth man ('having no special gift or scholastic genius ... but who covered all the angles and applied himself,' according to a school friend) had been toiling usefully and honourably away in the Far East for thirteen years, much like a good colonial administrator of the last century, only to find the hounds of the press suddenly breaking his door down and trying to photograph his wife.

On the other hand, the press and the larger world, were obscurely surprised to discover that Britain's highest-paid man was not a property speculator, or a white goods entrepreneur, but a man in spectacles who seemed to do nothing big enough or rash enough to make over £2.5m a year. He didn't live in a mansion. He drove a Mercedes. He had no vices, other than keeping a few race horses. He didn't fit the bill. Christopher Heath peered out at the world in a condition of modest surprise (flattering of them to pay me this attention, no idea why they should bother, though . . .) while the world peered back at him, looking for the riches of Croesus and finding only a £30,000 saloon car.

The mechanism behind this stupefying wealth was a securities firm which specialized in Japan and the Pacific Basin. Originally an outfit with ten people in London and five in Tokyo, it was bought outright by Barings in 1984, swelled into a 370-person organization with offices in Hong Kong and Singapore, and went on unostentatiously doing business (like a quoted £300m stock market deal for a Hong Kong property company, which would have netted the firm perhaps £1m in straight fees). Christopher Heath's annual salary was in fact, £100,000. The rest came from profit-sharing.

What made it worse was the fact that he got into it by chance: a dinner-party conversation alerted him to Japan. Before that, he'd been a stockbroker's analyst, specializing in hotels. He had no names, no relations, no tricks to pull. A banker said, 'He's a straight, hard-working young man who happens to be . . . *in the right place at the right time. It could have been any number of others; it just happens to be him.*'

The causal connection between the earner and the income seemed wrong. We're all, we like to imagine, straight and hard-working. We might think of ourselves as diligent, professional, shrewd, full of expert knowledge. But we don't get £2.5m. We don't even know how to start. We never even get to the place where that kind of luck, or magic, hangs around.

Unless we go to the City: that's where the normal connection between genius and wealth, or grit, or charisma, or *panache*, and wealth breaks down. Of course! The best-paid man in the country had to be something in the City, even if he went to Japan to do it! The City's where the laws of our financial universe get thrown out of the window. It's alchemy. 'People were and still are,' Lucky Paul confesses blandly, 'indecently rewarded . . .'

HOW TO GET CAUGHT

Lucky Paul, Keith the Computer Demon, and thousands of graduates like them, trusted in the City in its mood of Big Bang super-abundance, to turn their quotidian cleverness into real wealth. Christopher Heath was the unassuming apotheosis of a system. But sometimes the alchemy blows up. If Sir James Goldsmith was an alchemical genius who could magic money out of the air, then Geoffrey Collier was a druggist who overheated the retort. He went from head of securities business with Morgan Grenfell (and an income of what? £100,000? £200,000? £300,000 a year?) to expulsion from the Stock Exchange, a suspended prison sentence and a £25,000 fine at the Old Bailey. At the same time that Sir James Goldsmith was creating money without any kind of tricks, dodges, or hidden wires, Geoffrey Collier (whose act was *all* tricks, dodges and hidden wires) was watching the equipment explode in front of him. He formally resigned from his job on 10 November 1986, after being interviewed by Morgan Grenfell's compliance officer and three directors. How could he have gone wrong so appallingly?

It involved the takeover of an engineering group called AE, who were trying to avoid being absorbed by another company, called Turner & Newall. Towards the end of October, Robert Maxwell decided to make his own bid for AE, and set Morgan Grenfell to work for him. Clearly, anyone holding shares in AE on the day that a great plutocrat such as Robert Maxwell announced his interest in them, would be holding a profit: the more someone like Robert Maxwell wants your shares, the more they're worth. There was a team meeting at Morgan Grenfell on the afternoon of 2 November. They were going to announce the Maxwell bid on the following morning. Overnight, a company which Geoffrey Collier controlled, bought up 50,000 AE shares for £118,000, through a Los Angeles stockbroking firm. An hour after the Collier purchase was safe, Robert Maxwell made his bid known to the rest of the world.

The price of AE shares went straight up from 236p (roughly what Collier paid) to 267p. Collier went on and netted a profit of around £15,000 and that was that.

Or it would have been, but for the fact that someone at Chase Securities (how aptly named) got suspicious and told the Los Angeles stockbrokers, and by 6 November the Los Angeles stockbrokers had told Morgan Grenfell. Geoffrey Collier resigned four days later, asking that he might make his full confession in writing. The job went; so did the twenty-five roomed house in Kent and the red Porsche.

Why did he do it? What's £15,000 to Geoffrey Collier? It's unimaginable money to some junkie who goes shoplifting to pay for his habit, but to Collier it was just more money. And in the drab light of hindsight, the operation looks so obvious, so amateurish. If this was insider dealing, then it was absurdly simple. Overstuffed brokers grumbled that Collier was a man who clearly went to the wrong school, and satisfied themselves with that. But what Collier did seems more like an unthinking reflex, a *tic* which you find many City people suffer from and which hardly arouses comment. It was a reaction to news which drove him from the team meeting to the telephone. It was the same kind of reaction that drives the City along every day of the year, and for which we pay our brokers and analysts and market makers all the time. Ideas, information, they're money. That's what people work with in the City. Collier relaxed for a moment, scrambling his personal self with his City self, mixing up the legitimate profit motive with the reflex of greed.

It could have happened to anyone; at least it could have happened to anyone in the City. While the Collier scandal was happening, two other takeover bids were going on: British & Commonwealth were bidding for a finance group called EXCO, while BTR were taking a knife to Pilkingtons, the glass makers. But while the Pilkington bid was much contested, the EXCO takeover was an agreed offer. Someone observed that in the month before the bid for EXCO (planned quietly by a handful of people behind doors with stout locks) was announced, the share price had dribbled down by 10 per cent. The Pilkingtons bid, however, was hostile, required a great deal of planning, and involved far more people, some of whom had big mouths or defective scruples or both, since the price of Pilkington shares went up by 15 per cent *before* the bid was announced.

Now, if you have access to £50,000, and someone who knows things comes to you and says that Pilkingtons are going to be looking at a hostile bid from BTR in three weeks' time, and your £50,000 is doing nothing special at the moment, then you may well despise yourself for not doing some business on your own account. And who could live with that?

HOW TO MAGIC MONEY AND NOT GET CAUGHT

There was another way to manage the trick of time, place and money, that involved no insider dealing, no personal fortunes, no special job in Hong Kong. It was the privatization programme. By December, British Gas was up for the asking.

For weeks, Lucky Paul had been telling people to acquire as many shares in British Gas as they could. He did it professionally (even though his speciality was electricals). He did it casually, when touring a CD warehouse, and the Managing Director had taken him by the elbow, off to a quiet corner of the stockpile and begged his advice. He found himself barking it over dinner with friends and their wives and their husbands. You *must* get in your applications! 'You're *mad*, just *mad* if you don't fill in your applications!' he yelled across the artichoke soup. He thought for half a minute about making some multiple applications for himself and his wife. He knew, just as everyone knew in the City, Demon Keith, Webb, the Ace Merchant Banker, everyone in the City knew that you had to have a piece of British Gas for December. It was a Christmas present.

Let's give Lucky Paul a father. Lucky Paul's father is, say, a retired doctor with an itch to invest. He reads *The Economist* and the *Financial Times*. Lucky Paul mails him research material from time to time. He has a little £15,000 portfolio which he watches over like an orchid. It's too expensive to job in and out of stocks all the time. The firms of little stockbrokers, even his local bank, want a fortune in commissions. So he sits on his little portfolio, and applies for some British Gas shares, and Paul's mother, who thinks of the Stock Exchange as a kind of pricey funfair in London, keeps out and won't contemplate the British Gas Christmas present. 'You're mad,' Lucky Paul insists down the phone. 'Fill in the application form.'

It was a present, precisely because it had nothing much to do with the Stock Market. The British Gas sell-off, like British Telecom, and Jaguar and the TSB, was a government lottery. Provided you got some shares when they were handed out, and provided you sold them again, fast, you were going to make money. The only doubt in the operation hung over whether or not you would get the shares. It was democratic because anyone could take part. You didn't have to be a special. You could work and live in Selkirk, and you were as well placed as Lucky Paul. All you needed was some loose cash and the desire to go gambling.

The government let an ad. agency called Young & Rubicam sell the product. The idea was to pull in more from the C2 and D social classes, the yob classes, the underpaid, the credulous and the lower-middle-class. This was what was known as Popular Capitalism: the closer approximation of the City's desires with the yearnings of a bus driver or a nursery school helper. But even the doltish public knew what privatizations were for. They were for making a profit in no time at all.

So Young & Rubicam, with the help of a £25m expense account, evolved a campaign of such cretinizing insistence that you would have to have been dead not to have spotted that the old Gas Board was up for sale. For what seemed like a lifetime, we got short TV commercials, big TV commercials, billboard posters, newspaper ads, radio ads, commercial breaks in our *dreams* where this guy called Sid was hunted across cities and villages by a nation of character actors ('If you see Sid, tell him. Do tell Sid. Hurry up, Sid!'), but never materialized to send off for his prospectus or application form. It was like *Waiting For Godot*. That and the City pages of the broadsheet and tabloid newspaper, conspired to beat our brains to powder. We had to apply. In fact the only beauty of the 'Tell Sid' campaign was that it blew up on its own relentless tiresomeness. Although 7.5m investors registered an interest in buying British Gas shares, by the time it came to put up the cash, only 4.5m could be bothered. The rest were so distracted with irritation that they kept their money under the bed.

Those who marshalled their rage against Sid, and got some shares, did well. You could have paid 50p a share, and sold it on the first day of trading, for a clear 17p profit. More than 1bn British Gas shares were traded on the Stock Exchange within the first two days of dealing, by people keen to collect. Even if you'd dithered until the end of the week, there was still a premium of 14p a share. It was a gift. It was also a gift for the government, who took £5.4bn.

The word 'stagging' came up all the time. It was the third thing you had to do, to win in the lottery: you had to sell your shares the moment you received them. It wasn't share ownership at all. The last thing you wanted was to own the things. So you stagged. This is a delightful word, mediaeval in its suggestion of the hunt, the leaps and starts of the beast. And if some thrilled cabbie from Solihull actually took £1000 out of his Post Office savings account, spent it on Gas shares and sold them on day one of trading, then for that moment, he was a City spirit. What he'd enjoyed was an hour of magicking money from nothing; the bringing together of circumstances, luck and greed, to conjure gold from thin air. It was hardly an insider deal; it was the most public of deals. But it had the insider deal's no-loss certainty, action based on news, a tip-off which was as loud and big as the launch of a ship, but a tip-off all the same.

And if you'd been Geoffrey Collier, and you knew with as much certainty as you knew anything that shares in AE were going to go vertically upwards, and you'd been able to magic something out of thin air, if you'd been him . . .

There is a difference! Lucky Paul would complain. Collier didn't *need* to do it. He should never have contemplated it. There are things that you don't do. First of all, because if you get caught, it makes everyone else look so silly . . . 'No! First of all, because we get paid,' agrees Lucky Paul, 'for our legitimate services – we get *over*paid for our legitimate services . . . and there has to be a relationship of trust between the City and the public it serves. It's not hard to draw the line: stagging your British Gas shares is simple opportunism. But Collier was out of court whichever way you looked at it.'

CHRISTMAS

Lucky Paul and his wife made a profit out of Lucky Paul's British Gas shares. Lucky Paul's father missed out.

Better than that, was the end-of-year bonus from the firm. It took Lucky Paul's income headily closer to six figures, and when he went out on the first of three lunchtime piss-ups in the Christmas week, he felt arguably, wonderful.

The Jamaica Inn (with its hideous amber light and a map of the world stuck upside-down over the bar) was jammed with City folk, their faces burning with alcohol and excitement. Simpson's restaurant (address: a roguish 38½ Cornhill) banked up the open furnace which it maintains even in the foulest August days, and grilled a slaughterhouse of chops and steaks. The Pavilion wine bar was rent by yappings and howls and regurgitations and men and boys shouting, while one or two haggard seniors tried to explain to their mistresses that they had to spend Christmas with the wife and kids.

The graph of London's bull market in share prices was pointing at the sky with such virility, that you couldn't believe that it wasn't going to go through 2000 on FOOTSIE before very long. Big Bang had settled down, it seemed. There were an awful lot of people around, and they were being paid outrageously, and there were yobs from Chingford and Dagenham and East Ham who worked as equities dealers, or foreign exchange traders, or on the London International Financial Futures Exchange, and who took home £150,000 and had the manners of goats, but it was all right. And there was no reason to look beyond the next fortnight into any kind of black world of retrenchments or losses or redundancies.

There was also a man called Ivan Boesky. Back in 1985, he'd already attracted enough notoriety for *Time* magazine to run a piece on him. He was, it turned out, a professional arbitrageur, a once-poor, lived-over-a-delicatessen-immigrant's-son from Detroit, who speculated on share price movements for a living. To this end, he worked a 160-line telephone system, employed 100 permanent staff as analysts and information gatherers, and kept tabs on business developments with a militia of independent tipsters. 'This is not,' he said, 'some kind of gambling exercise. It's a very serious business.'

Of course, it was both a gambling exercise and a very serious business. It was spectacularly serious: Boesky had made $50m in 1984, when Texaco took over Getty. He'd also earned $65m in the same year when Chevron had bought out Gulf. In 1985, he'd been holding 3m Holiday Inn shares at $47.30, at the point when Holiday Inn offered to buy them back at $49.00. In some ways, it could have been the City's dream operation, fusing hard intellection with gambling instinct. His personal fortune was put at around $150m. He was caked with money. He drove around New York in a stretch limousine that looked like a missile transporter.

And there he was, photographed at his desk, a glass ashtray in front of him big enough to hold a human head, and he was winking at the *Time* camera, and leering, like some sort of poisoned horse.

A year later, he was being charged with insider trading (after his buddy, Dennis Levine had grassed on him), and had passed on a sackful of material to the US Securities & Exchange Commission, who in November 1986, passed it on to the DTI, who in December, had started to investigate the Guinness company. One or two people in the City, that Christmas, felt their stomachs churn whenever they passed a policeman.

3

JANUARY 1987: THE UNCOMFORTABLE NEW WORLD

The Temple of Mithras and the NatWest tower; the Bank of England and Salomon Brothers' dealing floor ('the largest in the *world*, bud'); the meshing of the old and the new ... You could find a nicely tortured example of the grinding of the new City gears, in Lloyd's, the insurance market. This institution is almost the City inside the City, with its confusion of prejudices and ambitions and Sacred Monsters. It does its richly valuable business unbothered by the banks or broking houses, much as the City used to do, when it veiled itself from the rest of the country. But, like the City as a whole, it also stares dumbly at two pressing contingencies: the law and the future.

THE LLOYD'S MAN

We might think of Nick as in his mid-thirties, married, doing nicely at Lloyd's. He could have spent Christmas in the country with his in-laws, then gone skiing for a week, then returned to work, brown as a nut and full of zest. The month went on, and Lloyd's, away from the Bull Market and new technology, did its business as usual in Richard Rogers' anodized thinking machine.

Then, on 22 January, the DTI published the Neill Report on Lloyd's. This was a huge document, which pointed out three main shortcomings in Lloyd's practices (no register of agents' charges; a bad standard underwriting agency agreement; the practice of running parallel syndicates), and recommended a number of smaller changes. Now, it wasn't just that there was this report headed by Sir Patrick Neill, and it made this or that recommendation: it also reminded the world that Lloyd's (the crankiest and most profitable single institution in the City) was full of, what? Imperfect traditions? Ways of doing business that you might object to if they were done to you? Malpractices? And if anyone had time to refocus from the FOOTSIE, they might have been prompted to wonder how many straightforward people there were at Lloyd's, and whether they all knew one another personally.

Even for the City, Lloyd's is a bizarrely introverted institution. The City's natural gift is to take services and functions and isolate them in pockets of overgrown specialization. So gilts brokers don't know about the options traders on the next floor down; foreign exchange dealers haven't the remotest idea what goes on in the corporate finance department next door; and no one knows what Lloyd's really does or how it makes so much money (over £20m of premiums are taken by Lloyd's every day).

Everyone holds an opinion though. Lloyd's is inward-looking to the point of suffocation. Lloyd's is the last resort of the witless toff: if you're too stupid to get a job in the City, go and work at Lloyd's. ('This is a filthy lie,' says Nick, hotly. 'There are some damn clever people working here. I meet them every day.') Lloyd's lives in a madhouse designed by a practical joker. Lloyd's can never get clean. Anybody will say something about Lloyd's, even if it's only to pass on what someone else has said to *them*. There's something about Lloyd's that seems to provoke outsiders into abuse, or baffled hilarity – like the kid with bad skin and spectacles who gets beaten up in the playground just by standing out of everyone's way.

At least, that would be true if Lloyd's managed to mind its own business. But for years, it's been involved in a kind of anguished, recalcitrant self-surgery, news of which it sometimes blurts out to the rest of the world, or which the rest of the world makes it its duty to reveal. For the last ten years, much of the news centred on a person called Ian Posgate. Posgate was a Svengali of the cramped, preposterous Lloyd's inner world.

The first time he got into trouble was in 1970, when he was censured by the Committee of Lloyd's, mainly for exceeding his underwriting limits. Posgate was an underwriter who simply had to have a piece of the action, whatever it was. He was one of those bullet heads who sit at their underwriter's desks all day, waiting for a broker to arrive with a risk to be insured. The difference with Posgate, the thing that makes Lloyd's people still shiver with nostalgia, was the way he consumed business. 'Posgate was a *genius*,' says Nick the broker, quite seriously and without a vestige of self-consciousness. 'If you'd ever seen him underwrite a risk — it'd take him a couple of seconds sometimes, then *bang*! That'd be it!' The bang was Posgate accepting a piece of the risk on behalf of his syndicate and earning it (and himself) another fee. He didn't even wait to be approached. 'He knew which brokers would have something that he wanted, and he would grab them as they went past, and say, I'm in for *that* one.'

There is, however, a bourne set on how much underwriting you can do, and Posgate, lunging at every bit of profit that came near him, exceeded his limits. The Committee of Lloyd's took legal advice as to whether or not to refer him to the Director of Public Prosecutions, but learnt that they had no obligation to do so. So instead they got Posgate to join a firm of brokers called Alexander Howden, not acting as a principal, but under the control of the boss, Kenneth Grob. The idea was that the arrangement would calm Posgate into acting merely like any other ambitious underwriter. Even so, by the start of the 1980s Posgate was writing for about 6000 Names (the private individuals whose personal assets actually underwrite the risk insured) which was in effect over a quarter of the total membership of Lloyd's. He was also earning, so it was said, around £700,000 a year.

But as well as making a living, Posgate and the four directors at Alexander Howden (including Posgate's conscience, Kenneth Grob) were also filtering very large amounts of their Names' money through a network of reinsurance premiums, banks, companies registered in Lichtenstein and Panama, shareholdings and controlling interests. These eventually disentangled themselves into possessions like a £1.85m villa in the South of France, furnishings and fittings worth £150,000, and a number of expensive oil paintings. It was unbelievable. It was also not unique, since at around the same time, the PCW syndicates, run by a pair called Cameron-Webb and Dixon, and another firm called Brooks & Dooley, were also found to be misappropriating their Names' money. Although no one has ever discovered exactly how much the three groups of fraudsters took from their Names, one estimate puts the total at £55m.

In fact, the more anyone looked into Lloyd's, the more complicated it seemed. You couldn't tell where ethical behaviour started or ended or even what ethical behaviour at Lloyd's looked like. Quite apart from Posgate and PCW and Brooks & Dooley, there were things called 'baby syndicates' which were simply small, low-risk, super-profitable syndicates run privately for especially well-connected Lloyd's people. If you're, say, a Lincolnshire grain farmer who wants to be a member of Lloyd's, then you join a syndicate or possibly several syndicates, and the underwriter writes all kinds of insurance business for you, and if the insured things blow up, or burn down, or sink, or just go wrong in some way, then you pay the claim because that's what you do if you're a member, and you hope for a better year next year. But if you're a smart person and are in the right syndicates, and know the right people, then they will put you in a special Club Class syndicate, a baby syndicate, which will get first (and perhaps only) crack at the high-earning business, the business that's as safe as houses and worth a fortune, and will make sure that no one else, least of all the grain farmer, even hears about it. The most profitable baby syndicate was found to be paying out £8600 on each £10,000 share.

Besides that, there was no formal separation of brokers and underwriters. This meant that when a client took along his insurance proposition to his broker, the broker could simply take it along to an underwriter who was part of the same firm. No competition on fees. All the profits for the same outfit. The cost passed neatly back to the customer.

And the only people apparently responsible for keeping Lloyd's clean were the members of Lloyd's who formed the Committee. Who cared what you did? The committee was full of Lloyd's people who knew what Lloyd's was all about and understood things with a sympathetic insight that not everyone else could have managed.

Posgate was really a brilliant focus for the world's disbelief at the way Lloyd's did things. Nick tries to make it clear why it was that Lloyd's loved him, in its way. Posgate was even elected to the

Committee of Lloyd's in 1981 on a wave of grudging approbation. The most Nick can bring himself to say by way of criticism is that Posgate was a very strange guy. 'He was,' Nick insists, 'tremendously ethical. He had an absolutely unshakeable ethical code. The trouble was, it wasn't anyone else's ethical code.'

This sounds familiar. It's a refrain which runs through every extension of the City. The beauty of Lloyd's is that it can take an aspect of City life like this, and embody it with such gaudy excess. The sheer concentration of improper traditions, redundant hierarchies, and cheerful peculators in one institution was like a distillation of the City's imperfections. By the turn of the 1980s, Lloyd's couldn't help but attract an army of investigators. In 1980 Sir Henry Fisher, merchant banker and Master of Wolfson College, Oxford, produced a long report into self-regulation and the worth of the Committee. In 1982 Parliament passed a new Lloyd's Act, which embodied Fisher's main recommendations. At the end of 1982 an accountant called Ian Hay Davison was brought in to head a working party on Lloyd's accounting practices. Davison's previous starring parts (among other things) had been as a DTI inspector pursuing John Stonehouse in 1974 then, later on, investigating an £8m fraud at the Grays Building Society. He was then given the job of Chief Executive, grappling with Lloyd's temperamental incapacity to police itself reliably. And then there was the Neill report of 1987 (by this time Davison had resigned), still detailing improprieties and shortcomings and the apparent ineffectuality of all the 1982 legislation. Lloyd's couldn't shake the things off.

They'd tried their best to show a brighter face to the world by moving into the new building, officially opened just a couple of months before, by the Queen. They spent around £200m on the Rogers fantasy, in order to get out of the tedious Festival Hall-style building they'd been in before. They knocked down their old 1926 home, to make way for Rogers, in a heavily symbolic announcement of the new age. But with an equal sense of the power of the numinous, they left an archetypal City monument behind them. This is a triumphal arch from the 1926 building, classical, coffered, rusticated, inscribed with names, and cemented into the doomy steel buttresses of Rogers' machine. It goes nowhere. It is dark, tenantless, obscure and huge. It is the perfect City doorway. Passers-by stare at it. They can't understand why this massively pointless thing should exist.

But although the new Lloyd's building is as fabulous as a griffin, the problem remains that no one told Rogers what they actually do for a living at Lloyd's. If you went in without knowing the place's true function, you might guess that it was a . . . luxury abbatoir? A spaceship garage?

There aren't any windows. Or at least there are but they are of frosted glass so that you can't see out. They admit a kind of darkness from the outside on to the underwriters' floors, which in turn surround the inevitable City *atrium* where a Lloyd's beadle sits in Georgian red under the Lutine bell and two miserable-looking companions, also in eighteenth-century fancy-dress, tap messages into a computer. There's a kind of greyness in the air, the kind you might expect in a very old municipal swimming baths. The lights incorporated into the concrete ceilings are ostentatiously full of struts and plastic warts. They look, perhaps by design, like a jet engine at take-off. In fact, they're so inventively framed that by the time the light hits the ground below it's as dim as a pocket torch.

The Rogers bare metalwork, tubing, plumbing, piping and ducting writhe in and out of the building. The glass lifts (with more aircraft technology in the little red lights they bear on their lids) zip up and down the outside with their cargoes of queasy brokers and underwriters. The window cleaners' cranes peep out over the summit. The Lloyd's waiters stand on the steps, waiting to shoo you away.

They hate the new Lloyd's building. Lloyd's bitterness at the new Lloyd's building stands as a paradigm of the whole City's distaste for the technology of the future. Nick loathes it with the kind of loathing that doesn't know where to start first: 'When you think what they *could* have done with £200m. The place is a *club*. It's a place where members might come only once a year. All right, but they want to say, "I'm coming up to Lloyd's, let's meet there." And *this* is what they get . . . The Captain's Room (the Lloyd's restaurant), where do you think that ought to be? On the top floor? It's in the basement. The café – Lloyd's *started* as a coffee-house – should be a

54

terrific café. Now they sell the worst coffee in London. At the ILU (the Institute of London Underwriters), they have an *excellent* café. You can get breakfast in there at eight o'clock, so all the brokers go over there for breakfast and they stay there, especially if it's raining, all day. We're losing business to the big firms this way . . .'

The building reveals the rupture between modern times and Lloyd's unregenerate clinging to the nineteenth century. The exterior is amazing – it springs bizarrely out at you like no other building in the City – but inside it's like a Victorian activity painting, like Hicks' *The General Post Office –1 Minute to 6*, or Frith's *The Railway Station*. It's a scene of unending, crowded human activity, filled with the kind of demented purposefulness you associate with nineteenth-century London. Toffs, yobs, damp young men with badly-cut hair, women made up to look like Brazilians, fat boys, degenerating lechers, Smart Alecs in snug-fitting double-breasted suits and waxy ties, lads built like jockeys and wearing Norman Wisdom jackets, all hurry around Richard Rogers' irrelevantly brilliant machine for thinking. The diversity and sheer bustle of the enterprise make your head swim. And what confirms the feeling of living history – of a process whose currency was minted two hundred years ago – is the prosaic fact that they *still* do what they've *always* done. The underwriters still sit at boxes whose dimensions intentionally recall the size and shape of an eighteenth-century coffee-house booth. They're still approached by brokers carrying bushels of chits, documentation, slips, folders, scrap paper who perch on a little chair set aside at the ends of the underwriters' desks and solicit business.

Each desk (or two or three) is occupied by a different underwriting syndicate which has to keep its records and reference books in the narrow space in the middle which isn't encroached upon by working underwriters or their assistants. So (and this is where the scene gets really fantastical) they build up little towers of shelving to hold the paperwork. The towers are sometimes no more than a couple of storeys high, but others go up for four or five tottering levels, each crammed with volumes of marine law or tonnage statistics or packets of 'necessary documentation' or diaries or almanacs. The engineering of these shelf towers jeeringly rebukes Rogers and his aesthetics of pure structure. The things are bolted together, nailed down, welded, bodged. They look deadly. Their apexes are always ready to cascade down at any moment, flattening the underwriter on his own biro.

Meanwhile, *below* the tower of knowledge, there is a deep trench, a kind of hold, filled with volumes of past underwriting agreements, bound in armoured metal books. These, Nick says, arresting you with a glitter of pride in his eye, are in fact very modern things. Lloyd's had to create a special kind of photocopier that could simultaneously copy and shrink the standard underwriting slip and eject a little facsimile, which then goes into the armoured binders but which takes up a quarter of the space of the real thing. Brilliant! So resourceful! But the whiff of Victorian London comes right back at you as you observe the jockey-sized lads in their two-for-a-tenner jackets diving into the underwriter's hold to drag up one of these glinting binders *on the end of a piece of string*. The bristling towers loom above; the hold full of armoured knowledge lies below. Lads jump up and down, hauling ledgers on strings. Secretaries and porky retainers pore over concertinas of paperwork . . .

'All right,' says Nick, losing his temper, 'what about *that* one?' He jabs his finger at an underwriter's box which has virtually no visible paperwork, no leaden superstructure, only little winking TV screens. Yes! TV screens just like the real world outside (for so the rest of the City has now become). The last quarter of the century rushes back in a flood of recognition. But the drawback is that none of the computers can communicate with each other. When some underwriters decided to buy in the technology, they all bought different systems. Now Lloyd's Committee can see that if all underwriters were computer-linked to the same system, they might decimate the bushels of paperwork which are lugged across from floor to floor every minute of the day and which give the place its furious Frith-like character. But the underwriters have already invested their money. They don't want to buy another new machine with new and difficult software. So the computer installations wink away to themselves and the paperwork piles up across the room.

And yet the figures are modern: a regular underwriting box, one of these working history lessons, can, with a staff of eight or ten, have an annual turnover of £28m.

*

Lloyd's is a close society. It doesn't forgive easily. When the Queen opened the new building on 18 November 1986, Ian Hay Davison, the troublesome accountant, was not invited. For the time that Davison was Chief Executive, he was put up with; he was a sanctioned messenger from the outside. He had things to tell Lloyd's that could ease its progress in the future. 'I think,' claims Nick, 'a lot of people in Lloyd's simply didn't realize they were doing wrong. When Davison was sorting things out, he had these things we called "The Davison Roadshow" — that's pretty ripe, actually . . .' These were seminars in which the cruel accountant sifted through such tasteless matters as agency, trust, the relationship between client and professional. 'We all came out saying, well I've certainly done *that* in my time . . . We did things without *really appreciating what we were doing . . .'*

But Davison got tired of butting his head on Lloyd's un-regeneracy, and left. Davison was, in the end, different. It just doesn't work if you start to have too many rules, the Lloyd's people say. *Leave us alone.* We're making a profit. What more do you want?

Lloyd's, the City within the City . . . 'We did things without really appreciating what we were doing . . .' No one would think of Nick as a criminal. If Nick ever volunteered to perform an immoral act, it would be something like wearing his wife's brassière under his dinner jacket for a joke; or thieving an ashtray from a foreign restaurant. It's not even that Nick is too stupid to imagine an authen-tic, intentional, wrong act. It's more that his view of the world has never had that much room for gross moral turpitude. We can see him, with Lucky Paul, going to a boy's public school in provincial England: the sort with a multicoloured brick chapel as cold as a lavatory, senior masters who wear their copious wartime decorations on Speech Day, a hugely expensive and unreliable modern language laboratory, lodged schismatically in the oldest building in the school and which regularly mutinies against the language master's com-mands. From there, father knows a man in Lloyd's, the man in Lloyd's shows Nick around, gives him lunch and Nick joins up. He's never exposed to outside influences. Lucky Paul enjoys the gentle dis-traction of goading Nick's tight-sphinctered Toryism. How could he be bad?

At the same time, how can he parade his yearning admiration for Ian Posgate, the single most visible renegade in the whole Lloyd's building? Well, if the guy's a real professional, you can't take that away from him. Bang! There goes another piece of the action with Posgate's name on it. He was a great, mad, underwriter. You can't disguise your feelings about that. Yes, he was too successful, in the way that megalomaniacs tend to be, shortly before they stop being successful. Of course, Nick agrees, Posgate was involved in fraud, in criminal activities, yes. That's the price you pay sometimes. Genius goes hand-in-glove with madness. And in this case, madness goes hand-in-glove with impropriety. It's tempting to complete the syllogism and just say that genius in the City goes hand-in-glove with impropriety. Posgate was in a tradition of arrogant City mavericks, men who pushed things too far, who made it happen in an old, free City way. He was perhaps too zany in some respects, but he was at least an individualist, not an accountant or a pen-pusher with a clearing bank. If you admired Posgate, as many did, you were admiring a tradition of anarchic City practice, now dying in the fusillade of Fisher reports and Lloyd's Acts and Neill reports.

As for his own technical imperfections, lit up by the Davison Roadshow, for these Nick pleads ignorance. You can't hound a chap when he doesn't appreciate the misdemeanour he's committing. And it's no good coming up with that crack about it being your duty to know exactly where your duties lie and what legal and moral restraints there are on you, because there simply aren't enough hours in the day to keep up with *everything* and, what's more, it's made worse every time a Fisher report emerges or a Neill report pops out, because it only leads to deadweight legislation which makes things more time-consuming, inefficient and, finally, not good for the customer. And that's the last thing *anyone* wants. Just think what would have happened if there'd been a Neill report on all the rest of the City. Think of the bill-drafting and statute-surgery and clause-building *that* would entail. The rest of the City gets off lightly. We know what goes on there.

What was going on, exactly? The City seemed to be in a condition of progressive character disintegration. There was one City which looked jaunty to the point of vacuity; and one hunted, grim City that peeked out from behind the hilarity.

On the one hand, by mid-January, the FOOTSIE had broken through the 1800 mark for the first time in its life (on Friday the 16th, at lunchtime), while the Dow Jones Index had gone through 2000 for the first time in its life. People observed that the Stock Market had been on the longest undeviating upward run that anyone could remember. The mood was that things were going to go up further, even though the FOOTSIE dropped back into the 1790s for the rest of the month. Lucky Paul found it onerous to build the nut of professional caution into his sector surveys, but forced himself to all the same.

On the other hand, there was the Guinness scandal. The plot of Guinness was so mangled and incomplete at this stage that it was hard to know anything other than the biggest, clearest facts – like Roger Seelig's quitting Morgan Grenfell, and Ernest Saunders' quitting Guinness. But Guinness had taken over the Distillers company, with Ernest Saunders as the Guinness Caesar and Roger Seelig as, well, hardly Mark Antony, but supposedly enjoying a similarly confident and inclusive association. Then Boesky had given a crate of testimonies to the SEC, who passed them to the DTI and the DTI were looking at how Guinness had swung the battle for Distillers. Something unaccountable seemed to have been going on with the Guinness share price during the takeover bid. Roger Seelig, the takeover genius from Morgan Grenfell, would know about unaccountable share price movements. He resigned at the very end of December 1986. Saunders resigned from the board of Guinness just over a week later.

The City's view of Morgan Grenfell's corporate finance team was that they'd made Morgan Grenfell the absolute masters of the takeover by *using every inch of the playing surface*. It wasn't that they didn't have all the probity and address that merchant banks were meant to have; just that, from time to time, they seemed to be able to enjoy a kind of philosophical detachment from it. Roger Seelig, with his Tudor courtier's face and his weirdly crimped hair, was either (depending on where you stood) a merchant banker of real flair, or a mad cultist, a man who saw himself as a six-footer among pygmies.

If you were Webb, he simply aroused loathing. 'He was tremendously vain. All that coiffured hair and immaculate appearance . . .' Some City people regard a lively interest in your wardrobe as proof of a mired soul. Webb's suits are made for him, but he bags the trousers out at the knee, fails to dislodge the scurf around the collar, likes to jam his hands into his jacket pockets on cold days. He and Lucky Paul share the characteristic of wearing good clothes as if they were charity-shop gifts. Webb is also something of a company man, a team player, in his bilious way. Seelig, on the other hand, 'Really only lived for one thing, which was his self-aggrandisement. At Morgan Grenfell, they were all struck dumb when Seelig resigned. They all thought he was Jesus Christ.'

The Ace Merchant Banker, conversely, has too much respect for Seelig, the man who got things done. As with Nick, the Lloyd's man, and his stifled worship of Posgate, there's something about Seelig that can overwhelm scrupulous distaste. It makes for a troubled meeting of passion and philosophical restraint in the Ace Merchant Banker's soul. Even the Ace Merchant Banker, who writhes under the burden of his admission, has to make room for Seelig somewhere. 'He was good . . . the Dixons–Currys battle . . . the trick about buying up Distillers brands. Didn't work, of course, but at least he *thought* of it. He gave it his imaginative intelligence.'

The Posgate parallel is strictly tangental. Posgate and PCW made free with their clients' money. Some things are a matter of judgement (like excessive underwriting), others straightforward ethics (like depriving another person of his property). Seelig was engulfed in bids and deals which – as the Ace Merchant Banker points out – would give you no time for reflection, no room for uncluttered moral thought. But Seelig, like Posgate, was a charismatic City type, an individualist. And as the City became bigger, more international, organized by Americans and Japanese thousands of miles away down a telephone wire, as it shuffled gingerly into the light of exposure and legislation, as it became more and more like a multinational business than a collection of individuals, then the more Seelig started to look like a genius trapped in an amber of sudden change. He was up to date with his working practices; but mavericks were starting to look out of place.

Clearly, Roger Seelig was a driven being. He had no wife or children to bother with, preferring to live with his mother in a house in the Cotswolds, and could direct every bit of his personality towards work. In fact he embodied the common belief that anyone at the top had to have either an entirely free-form marriage or no marriage at all. By 1986, with Seelig's active participation, Morgan Grenfell were the *Mahdis* of company takeovers, with an involvement that year in £13.5bn's worth of business. Seelig also did a lot of smart, tyro things like run a fast car, do deals on a mobile telephone, wear Gucci shoes – things that Dennis Levine, or Ivan Boesky, would have understood and approved of. He was dynamic. And yet he was now buried in tittle-tattle concerning a letter written by Olivier Roux (one of the Guinness advisers), and the DTI inspectors emerging from Freshfields (the City solicitors who had advised Guinness during the fight) bent under the weight of 126 boxes of files and information, and a merchant bank called Henry Ansbacher who appeared to be holding some tainted money. So Seelig, the star of Morgan Grenfell, resigned.

The Director General of the Takeover Panel, John Walker-Haworth, said, 'I'm in a pretty nasty mood, as a result of Guinness!' This feeble interjection gave scope for the press's sarcasm, but it also pointed up in people's minds that somewhere a tough takeover battle had gone too far. Boesky and Dennis Levine had started the revelations in New York. Now, there was a whole cloud of transgressions waiting to rain on the City. On 22 January, Christopher Reeves, Morgan Grenfell's Chief Executive, and Graham Walsh, the bank's Head of Corporate Finance, both resigned. Jaws sagged. Reeves was the great man of Morgan Grenfell. He hadn't been part of the Guinness takeover job but, as chief executive, he had to carry the can.

Then, on 22 January, Lord Spens resigned from his job as Head of Corporate Finance with the merchant banking firm, Henry Ansbacher. No one knew what *he* knew, except that Henry Ansbacher had been involved in a dubious £7.6bn purchase of Guinness shares at the time of the takeover. The Bank of England, it was said, had leaned on Lord Spens. Lord Spens had to do his duty. He had to carry the can. This, of course, was only the start.

PROBLEMS

Now, the Big Bang and everything that led up to it didn't make the City any more agreeable. Lucky Paul stifles in his chipboard hutch. The dealers find themselves in batteries of workstations, in supermarket dealing rooms, a foot away from the armpits of their colleagues, and roped to a monomaniac TV screen. Even if you visit the Ace Merchant Banker at his multinational merchant bank, you'll find him in slave quarters. He says, come upstairs, I'll show you where I work. You compute his worth to the firm. It's high. His kinked gene lets him burn through the mathematics of exchange rates, forward markets, swaps, hedging, futures, all the unpleasant stuff involving the London Interbank Offered Rate which Lucky Paul runs from. You tot up his salary, the year's bonus, the company car, the BUPA payments and the cheap mortgage, and put him over the £100,000 a year mark. With all this you expect that the multinational will have given him, if not a panelled office, at least a room with walls and a carpet and a window.

But no. Instead, he gets a four foot by four foot space at the counter just like the dealers and salesmen. He has to be all these terrific things to the multinational, surrounded by telephones, shreds of paper, yobs, deadheads, and people who don't wash or shave adequately in the mornings. Where does he go for some peace and quiet? 'Aha,' he says, and you reckon, okay, he only uses the battery-pen desk once or twice a day. This is where we trudge down the corridor to the nice beige office. But he turns round to *another* four by four workstation: '*This* is where I go when I want some peace and quiet.' It looks exactly like the first one, except the paperwork's more profuse. That's what you get when they give you a directorship: two horrid places to work instead of one. The alternative, in some firms, is to have an angle of the room, three paces away from the nagging workstations, instead of a seat right in the middle. People have been drafted into banks and broking houses on vast salaries only to find themselves shown into the corner of a garage full of muttering savages.

It goes right through the City; the world of work shrivels to cubicles and battery pens. Now, dealers love to deal, wherever they are. There is nothing, they will tell you, quite like 'legging' your rivals 'over', whether it's in equity trading, gilts, financial futures, commodities or bonds. If you work on the floor of the London International Financial Futures Exchange, then you still do it by open outcry and you wave your arms about and jostle and yell. But elsewhere, the strain of gawping at a 14 inch TV in the battery pen week in, week out gets to even the hardest traders. They complain about their eyesight. It's got worse, you can tell it's got *markedly worse* over the time that you've been sitting in front of the screen.

Screen dealers work in spasms of energy. Much of the time, they slump into the dealer's posture with the arm cantilevered round the back of the head. They chew gum, toss bits of paper at each other, stand up and shout jokes and abuse. At other times, they collapse into a frenzy of work. Some kind of team leader pitches them into a particular stock, or the market blows up, or something happens somewhere which they need to track. Paunchy executives in their shirtsleeves use a bingo-caller's microphone to make announcements. The air gets hot and ripe. It's dealing, it's incredibly exciting (and stupefyingly dull when there's nothing to do). It can make you a lot of money, and you could as well be on the Cowley production line hanging car doors the way they lock you up at the workstation.

The opinion gatherers, MORI, ran a poll of jittery, stressed City folk in the year after Big Bang. Among other things, they claimed that 65 per cent of their respondents worried (with suitable reflexivity) about stress; that work hours lost through stress cost up to 3 per cent of a firm's wages; that you were more likely to suffer in a Big Bang-focused finance conglomerate than in a little house which stayed away from all the mergers. In fact, a research director for BUPA revealed that he'd been examining conditions in two banks. One, still small, unmerged, privately-owned, traditional, was staffed by paragons whose cigarette-smoking, drinking and coronary liabilities had all decreased. The other, consumed by a bigger firm before the Bang, had had management crises, walk-outs from its top executives, and hugely accelerating rates of drinking, smoking and corporate depression.

Not only that, but City people can't help but complain about the new hours they're working. No one likes arriving for Morning Prayers at eight o'clock, and staying until six in the evening. Sometimes it seems like nothing more than an especially redundant way of letting everyone else know you *work* for all that money you take home. There's a school of thought which blames it on the Americans and the Japanese. It's seen as an example of inexact thinking which presumes a direct link between long hours and hard work. You know what happens with them? They insist, argues the City old boy, that you work from 8 a.m. to 9 p.m., but in all that time no one actually *works*. Not hard. The Japanese especially are unbelievably inefficient workers. As a comparison, he dredges up a colleague, a dealer. He works very hard from 8.30 a.m. onwards but stops at 3.30 p.m. He gets home at 4.30 p.m. and slumps in an armchair for two hours before he can do anything, talk to his wife, say hello to the kids. Completely drained. That, the old boy insists, has got to be better than this frightful trend of working very long hours.

But the City's got a monkey on its back. We can do anything! We can work a 55-hour week, spend billions on computer equipment, frazzle ourselves in a barking stampede to get money, just like the Americans and Japanese! We overdid it in the past; we can overdo it now!

THE COMPUTER SHOW

The City has a technology obsession. It results in workstations, strained eyes, battery pens, millions of pounds of equipment. The compulsion of the new, as well as the fear of failure, goads it all the

time towards novelty-packed, depressing and exhausting ex-
penditures. It also means that each year now, there is an exhibition
called 'Computers in the City', aimed at the Demon Keiths of the
Square Mile and their progressively-minded bosses. It is a disturbing
event.

Computers are ambiguously friendly things. In the widest sense,
they can ruin you or make you zappingly efficient. But as tools,
things which sit on the desk (which are the desk in your modern
dealing room), they live in a zone somewhere between animate and
inanimate, clever and moronically obtuse. So a lot of 'Computers in
the City' is about software and systems, and sophisticated ways of
making the machine a comfortable extension of the person using it,
rather than a perverse, winking alien. But merely addressing this aim
calls up a nightmare of hashed chances and future disasters. Take
this, from a firm specializing in touch-sensitive computer TV systems:

> The next generation of high technology has arrived. When
> combined with a voice communication system, IBS provides a
> complete operating environment for dealers in foreign exchange
> and money markets. Each manager or dealer requires only a simple
> touch sensitive display screen and the telephone links. Gone for
> good are keyboards, walls full of video monitors for separate rate
> and news services, and scrawls on scraps of paper that can lead to
> million dollar mistakes . . .

The 'million dollar mistakes' bit is the clincher. It galvanizes the rest
of the patter into monstrous life. Who *hasn't* made a million dollar
mistake, once or twice in his career? And remember the weeks of
confusion, fear, shame, that followed the cover-up? But then, the
computer itself is a gamble, an act of blind faith, even a million
dollar mistake. Do we need a screen that you can carve up and
reshuffle into endless particoloured blocks with your fingers? Is there
any good reason why not? How far do we need to go with this Big
Bang thing?

Or do you want to skip the touchable screen altogether, and
concentrate on the software? What about Relational Technology's

INGRES 'a full functional relational database management and application development system that includes a sophisticated set of user interfaces . . . INGRES also supports the ANSII standard SQL query language . . .'? Now, this is meat and drink to Keith the Computer Demon, who tiptoes from stand to stand, shyly punching buttons and modestly enquiring after a system's powers, before turning away. ('I can do that already on our system, only better. I just like to know what the competition's up to.')

But it leaves Keith the Computer Demon as the conduit through which all his firm's technological ambitions must pass. Keith and a few of his colleagues understand VAX/VMS, MS-DOS, LISP-Architecture and SUN workstations, but in a firm of 850 people, it means placing big trust and irrecoverable money in a tiny minority. And each time the software consultancies and the hardware manufacturers yearningly extend their hands to the end user, they just aggravate the fear and tension that their very existence generates. For the 1987 show some stands tried to comfort you by lodging the avant-garde hardware in robustly familiar settings – a firm called NMW actually built a kind of neo-classical room, with pilasters and imitation marble, just like an old bank's main hall, out of which the little 14 inch TVs blinked keenly. The Stock Exchange's own stand tried to have it both ways, by constructing a very tangible, physical, steel rig (the familiar touch of stove-enamelled metal; the rigorous geometry of the future), but it was so low that anyone over 5 ft 6 in got his head stuck in the girders.

ICL, the British computer manufacturers, unwittingly caught the mood best, with a display entitled 'Illuminating The City'. You could see what they meant: the *motif* for the stationery and general graphics was a stylized, German Expressionist City, nothing but darkness and crazy angles, studded with flashes of lighted windows, indicating those very offices which were clever enough to use ICL computers; illuminating the City, in fact. But so much of the picture was black, infernal, gothic, that it looked as if ICL was a subsidiary of the *Nosferatu* software business. The City of tomorrow was black and insane. To make it worse, they draped the entire stall (one of the biggest there) in funeral banners, like the ones which came out for the death of George V.

There is also a devil, hidden in the system. Most of the money goes on smartening up the dealing floors and those parts of the organization which need to work with a lot of information at high speed. Only a little ever gets through to the back office, where contracted deals are finally given the bureaucratic treatment, and the paperwork is processed on settlement day. The back offices are still full of physical bits of paper, with drudges scrabbling through dividend slips, sold transfer forms, bought transfer forms, heaps of computer print-outs. The front of the house is magical, instantaneous, high-powered; the back is still a museum. It is an oversight which sits there, waiting to cause trouble.

But what do you expect? The very idea of newness is itself so new, that the City could hardly be expected to cover all the angles. Lloyd's bought itself a £200m building in which the nineteenth century soldiers gamely on. The Big Bang houses lashed out £4bn on computer novelties, but failed to automate the bit of the office that tied up the end of each deal. You really have to like the idea of progress you've embraced, to make it work. The City (snotty, hidebound, reactionary, short-term) found itself jerking upright out of a deep sleep, and in the confusion of abrupt wakefulness, could only blunder from target to target.

4

FEBRUARY: THE SMALL MAN

By now, the FOOTSIE had brightened up to 1800 and beyond. Morgan Grenfell's shares were looking unhealthy, but they were one of the exceptions. It was no time to have your money in the building society. Some more Americans were being arrested on Wall Street, from Goldman Sachs and Kidder Peabody, among others. Martin Siegel, a once-senior executive from Drexel Burnham Lambert, pleaded guilty to some insider trading charges and one or two tax evasion misdemeanours. He also settled a separate action from the SEC which had accused him of taking $700,000 in payoffs from Ivan Boesky, in return for stock tips. The money had, apparently, been delivered to him in briefcases bursting with notes.

But it was good, if you weren't, let's say, Martin Siegel. And one of the things which made it good, was the British Airways sell-off. It wasn't money in the bank in quite the same way that British Gas had been. The sale kept being postponed in the past, because BA couldn't make profits. Nor was it a great public monopoly. It had competitors. But like the other sell-offs, it was pitched cheap, at 125p a share, with only 65p to pay in the first instance. Also, the company might have been a dog in the past, but it was much less of a dog now. There was almost certainly a gift in there if you could get some shares.

PAUL'S FATHER: THE LILLIPUTIAN INVESTOR

Paul's father was right on top of things, once the close-print share application forms appeared in the daily papers. He was by this time utterly persuaded that popular capitalism was where his future lay. In his busy retirement, he was building an information slag heap of his own, a little mirror of his son's. There were new publications emerging for people like him. There were special interest magazines. There were bracing pocket textbooks for the amateur investor. Even the Stock Exchange turned out its own pleased-to-meet-you promotional material. And there were the *Daily Mail* and the *Daily Telegraph*, with their user-friendly financial sections, plus the *Financial Times*, with its strenuously complete (and really, narcotic) coverage of things that Paul's father had decided he should know about.

There's something uneasy, though, about this bringing together of the City with the Lilliputian ambitions of the individual. Its given name is popular capitalism, but this sounds too vigorous, too beefily democratic, for the world of intimate fears and bafflements which the small investor – Paul's father – inhabits.

The Economist, Money, Money Management, What Investment, Family Wealth, they are the emissaries into Paul's father's world. They line up in W. H. Smith's with the news from the Great Maw of Greed, and the good deals and the 'ones to watch out for'. And yet, for all their colour and excitement, there's something disappointing about them. It arises from the way their enthusiasm for the Unlisted Securities Market or Traded Options or whatever it might be, keeps compromising itself on a kind of fumbling matiness. *What Investment* magazine, for instance, runs a column called 'Joe Bloggs' (our Man in the City). Joe has the slovenly patter of an insurance salesman on the way down. He is billed as a 'Top Share Tipster', but he talks like this: 'Hang on for the ride,' he says. 'The Australian operators and Captain Bob [that is, the great plutocrat Robert Maxwell] are providing plenty of excitement! '. . . Those champagne sodden minds in the City . . . while I was drying out at a health farm in Sussex . . . all I can really do is blame my incompetent assistant . . .' Wealth Warning! it yelps at the top of the page. 'Readers should use the column as a guide for useful money making ideas and tips. Don't follow it religiously, the writer is often drunk!' What is it with Joe Bloggs? What kind of inadmissible nervousness sets him chattering away like this? Why the name Joe Bloggs, in the first place? What kind of confidence does it inspire? Why do they expect *us*, (scowls Paul's father, clicking his biro in and out furiously) to accept it? Even the graphics don't fit. Joe Bloggs is a cartoon, a giggling racketeer in a cheaply-drawn City suit. He's frequently depicted waving a glass of red wine at the reader.

It comes up again, in the DIY investment manuals that Paul's father sternly inspects in the backs of bookshops. There's a breeziness about them, a buttonholing slang, which would be incredible in a gardening manual or a cookery book. The same verbal attitudes recur. They're meant to comfort, ('They may be leading you up the garden path . . . all this may sound like marvellous fun . . . heigh-ho . . .') but they just irritate. Why do they need to do it? *Fortune International*, an American equivalent, doesn't patronize its readership with this sort of thing. It even looks serious, with its colour photographs and its smart layout. *What Investment* shares the same cheesy visuals as its advertisers: the PEP clubs run from rooms in W1; the Unit Trust outfits; the Penny Share tipsheets with their crushed, feverish full-page ads jammed with squabbling typefaces; the advisory services in Lancashire; the midget firms of stock-brokers.

If he were a typical retired investor, Paul's father (a surgeon perhaps, with some thirty years' standing in the community) would be used to better things. He would come from that part of society which has always had some interest in the Stock Market. Although statistically a part of the great army of 9.5m private shareholders which the Tory government sees as a capitalist evangelical movement, his background would place him with the old regime: over 60, socio-economic class B, more than four companies invested in. The evangelists are downmarket. In numerical terms, his class (the ABs) has gone from representing 56 per cent of all private shareholders in 1983, to around 29 per cent; while the C1s and the C2s now make up 60 per cent of all private shareholders, having had only a 38 per cent share back in 1983. It's the hairdressers and carpet salesmen and plumbers and taxi drivers, Lucky Paul's father concludes, who read *What Investment* and *How To Make A Killing In The Share Jungle*. They have to be Joe Bloggs' audience. Young folk (the twenty-five to forty-four up by 16 per cent; the fourty-fives to sixty-four down by 10 per cent) appreciate his elbow-squeezing style.

Even the Stock Exchange has got into the act, with its *Introduction*

To The Stock Market brochure. This is a small masterpiece of in-clusivity. Everyone is represented: the white Caucasian couple on page six are answered by the sloe-eyed chef on page twenty-two; the leathery construction worker in a hard hat counterpoints the juvenile laboratory technician; the blithe young family taking a walk in the garden anticipate the scrubbed wrinklies on the cover. There are arty-looking people and there are knuckleheads. There are tiny babies and people evidently about to drop dead. There is even a black man.

The text, meanwhile, is stiffly seductive. 'You might have sizeable assets but not much knowledge ... you might be someone who simply wants to make the occasional investment ... in between, of course, come most of us ...' And there *we* are at the foot of the page, walking the kid through a twinkling autumn forest. 'It's too often assumed,' nannies the booklet in the next paragraph, 'that brokers are only interested in the very rich investor. Don't believe it – and don't be put off. You'll find brokers helpful ...' Turn the page, and you're going for the big one. 'So You've Decided To Invest' bellows the *Introduction to the Stock Market*, and straightaway there's a terrifying heap of computer print-outs and stockbrokers' literature capped by an Ace Merchant Banker pocket calculator and an obsessively-sharpened pencil.

There is also a table of projected broker's charges on four typical share transactions. The text blurts out in a legalistic spasm: 'These figures, it should be emphasized, are only a guide.' Damn right, thinks Lucky Paul's father. It suggests that your local stockbroker will charge you a commission of no more than 1.5 per cent on the purchase price, plus VAT at 15 per cent and Stamp Duty at 0.5 per cent. Total cost of purchasing £1000 worth of shares – £22.25. But to a broker, the cost of executing a miniature share purchase or sale, is the same as the cost of a huge one. The documentation is the same. The call made on his back office where the settlements are logged up is the same. Who cares about some old boy from the west country who rings up with £800's worth of shares and an itch to call in his profits? And so, although plenty of small firms keen to look busy around Big Bang and the privatization boom, announced new, headily diminutive dealing costs, like 0.825 per cent on the first £7000 traded, or 1.20 per cent, or even 1.25 per cent, what do you know but their client lists are all full, or they demand a certain level of investment (more than a few thousands, I'm afraid) or they just never get back to you.

As the year wore on, a Labour MP called Tony Blair went the rounds of those stockbrokers listed by the Stock Exchange as specializing in the smaller investor. He had, admittedly, a ludicrously undersized transaction in mind; the sale of 200 shares in British Telecom, and that was all. But then, thousands of people did end up with birdseed like that after privatization. When he rang round his 151 self-elected small person's broking firms, he found that a third of them wouldn't sell the shares at all, a third wanted more than £20.00 to do it (which would have wiped out the annual capital gain on the shares), and out of the remaining fifty or so firms, only 36 would offer minimum commissions of less than £20.00.

The deal is merely a headache. A number of the bigger firms started up special small investor schemes early on only to drop them silently when it turned out that they were a waste of time and money. The high street banks stab away fitfully at the process, and Nicholas Goodison dredged up something called SAEF. This is nice: an acronym within an acronym in which the initials stand for 'SEAQ Automated Execution Facility', or perhaps more exactly, 'Stock Exchange Automated Quotations Automated Execution Facility'. Anyway, Sir Nicholas Goodison temptingly described it as the way ahead for small investors, an automatic, paperless system of dealing with share transactions, and one which (when it gets built) will halve the little man's costs.

Until then, Lucky Paul's father has to make do with the local bank and a charge of at least £20.00, plus VAT, plus Stamp Duty, whenever he wants to plunge into MK Electricals or Costain. That is, a minimum of £28.00, rather than the Stock Exchange's suggested £22.25 on a hypothetical £1000 purchase. Some people even reckon that you should allow as much as 10 per cent of the total transaction, to cover dealing costs. This is one reason why he looks on his little portfolio as a thing to live with, an addition to the scenery, rather than a roller-coaster of speculation. He occasionally yields to some imaginary investing in what seem to him (after all the month-old recommendations and disingenuous newspaper tips) like good propositions, and watches a fictitious high-return fund of £75,000 job in and out of the more exciting ventures, with only the lowest commissions shaved off by his fictitious broker at the end.

Lucky Paul's view of the small investor's prospects is sanguine. The way he sees it, the small man is well placed. 'Admittedly, the man in the street' (as he helplessly refers to his own father) 'can't know how the City feels about, let's say, Rocco Forte, in any detail; the City's bound to be ahead in some things. But the tipsheets and the press, they have a *lot* of stuff which is *right*. They really do. The jobbers read some of the tipsheets, themselves. They see a recommendation in there, they mark the price up straight away.' He pauses. The cause and effect he wants to illustrate seem to have led him into something of a bog.

Trying a slightly different tack, he argues that some of the newspaper columns, the *THROG ST.s*, the *What's Ups*, have a kind of prescience about them that he finds remarkable. They're almost too accurate, he says. They have information that – well, anyone could profit from. The small investor might have the impression that he's sitting at the far end of the chain of intellection that starts with people like Lucky Paul, but there are ways of shortening the chain.

Not only that, but some City people see it as their *duty* to be nice to nonentities. Lucky Paul actually tries to keep in touch with some of the firm's individual clients. Not that he telephones them with news of one of his electricals firms – that's reserved for the institutional investors and the fund managers. It's more passively friendly than that. Now and then, someone of unusual force of character, or simple craziness, gets past the broker out in the private investors' department, and through to an analyst like Paul, for a good sifting of his latest figures and projections. 'I like to keep in touch with individual clients,' Paul insists. 'I think the City can be too *distant* in its dealings with people.' Is this a tendril of Lucky Paul's socialism creeping around the frame? Is it a murmur of demotic recidivism? Is it Paul's aimless good nature? Whatever, Paul takes offence if you suggest that it makes him a rarity, a philanthropist among the greedy. He's not alone, he says. There are a number of people like him who take the private investor seriously and who will answer the phone even if it's a market gardener or garage mechanic with what Lucky Paul unthinkingly calls 'a piffling £5000 portfolio', on the line.

Elsewhere, there is a different view. This states that the City runs on information, some of it philosophically extremely close to inside information. The closer it is to inside information, the more it's worth. It also states that this information is never going to get to the private investor before it gets to the big investors or to the dealers. Therefore, the small investor is out of the picture. The cynic's response to the view that many newspaper columnists are well placed to get valuable commercial news, and that sometimes they get it before the rest, is that the journalist in question will often tell the analyst that he's putting in a paragraph about Amalgamated Consolidated Plc or whoever, on Sunday, and the analyst will go back to his office to tell the dealers who will promptly buy up the stock on Friday afternoon as fast as they can, and put a mark-up on it. 'By the time the retired major in Berkshire gets through to his broker on Thursday,' laugh the sceptics, 'he's completely out of date.'

You also have to ask yourself, which of these two scenarios is the more plausible. First, that the private client either gets a phone call from his broker, announcing some big news and calling for instructions to buy; or picks the analyst's posted report off the doormat, reads it carefully enough to spot the reasons advanced for buying up Amalgamated Consolidated Plc, has time and energy enough to get through to his broker and places an order.

The second scenario is that one of the firm's analysts writes a fervent recommendation for a company. This is circulated to the dealers, the institutional salesmen, the fund managers and big institutional investors. They buy up the shares in large amounts through the broking firm that made the recommendation. At the end of the list, the house's private clients (those with enough money to warrant getting any news at all) are circularized. Then, when the buying's done, anyone else may have it, by which time it seeps down to the small man who buys dear if he buys at all.

And then you have to ask yourself, what does it benefit the stockbroker, that he should encourage the attentions of investors with £1000 ambitions? Why should he need them at all? Viewed as a business proposition, a small investor has very little going for him. He's unlikely to become a big investor. He's unlikely to know any big investors whom he can recommend to the broker. And even if he does know any big investors, they will already have made their arrangements. The most you can say for it, is that it encourages a broadening of goodwill towards stockbrokers. But stockbrokers have lived without the community's goodwill (in fact, with the community's leery disapproval) for decades; why should they want to cultivate it now?

The thing has come out backwards. Appealing to small investors is an idea in action — but an idea which stumbled out to fill a need that no one is certain exists. Sheer force of circumstance brought it into being. The Government had the notion of cutting its losses and taking in some once-in-a-lifetime funds, by selling off the nationalized industries. Then, it turned out that the City was, at the same time, in the throes of reinventing itself and becoming dynamically populist. The thrust of privatization met with the philosophical ambitions of the City, and popular capitalism grew awkwardly out of the two. The difference from regular Conservative Government and City practice is that popular capitalism is an idea looking for a consumer, rather than a brutalist way of making the best out of what you've got. But since the City and the Tory party have to work together to survive, and since popular capitalism has more immediate attractions than popular socialism, the City took the idea on board. Of course now it doesn't know what to do with it. It's a nice idea, but not a business proposition. It's one of the more original aspects of the shambling City revolution. The implications could be enormous. But the City would be far happier with popular capitalism if it meant no more than a proletarian reflex of approbation for everything the City did. It loses its charm when provincials ring you with their tens of British Gas shares and expect you to do something about them.

Maybe this helps to explain the awkwardness with which the investment magazine experts address the lay public. If they were more certain of their reasons for addressing them at all, they might do it better.

*

It does not bother Paul's father though. His perspective is *so* small-time that for the moment simply being involved is quite exciting enough. And something like the British Airways sell-off is the greatest fun, being straightforward, respectable gambling.

He examined the gargantuan application form which appeared in his *Sunday Telegraph* at the beginning of February 1987. It was an offer by Hill Samuel & Co. Ltd. on behalf of the Secretrary of State for Transport of up to 720.2m Ordinary shares at 125p a share. There was a wall of *minutiae* which followed, about restrictions and conditions, printed so small that his eyes hurt. Dealings, it announced, would commence on the Stock Exchange at 2.30 p.m. on Wednesday, the 11 February 1987. That's what really set the blood racing around Paul's father's head; the prospect of dealings, and selling the things and stagging. And to heighten the minute illicitness of the pleasure, there was also a warning. 'Only one application may be made for the benefit of any person. Criminal proceedings may be instituted against anyone knowingly making or authorizing more than one application for the benefit of any person.' Then there was the table of permitted share applications, which was the only thing he could make out without difficulty. He put himself in for 1000 shares at 65p part-paid.

Paul's mother was still a step behind Paul's father. By the time she'd absorbed the significance of British Gas, she was ready for another identical privatization (a vast public utility, with an unanswerable monopoly) but not for British Airways which was fraught with devilish possibilities. She contented herself with a handful of barbs over the morning toast.

THE ACE MERCHANT BANKER AND THE CRISIS OF DOUBT

Towards the end of February, Lucky Paul and the Ace Merchant Banker have lunch at Bentley's in Bishopsgate.

Immediately behind Paul and the Ace Merchant Banker, a trio of brokers is laying into the wine and peanuts. 'You bastard!' they cry delightedly at each other. 'I was so drunk. You know? Completely ratarsed. Fell through the front door, two in the morning, pitch dark. Staggered to the bog, and psssshhhhh! All over the place! What a purler! God, the wife went out of her mind! Thought I was a fucking rapist!'

A pair of youthful toffs lodge themselves at the next table. One of them wears his hair smacked down on his scalp with oil, a double-breasted dark blue suit with a motorway chalkstripe running brilliantly up and down it, a shirt with the collar cut back to reveal more of the deft shirtmaker's seaming around the neck, and shoes with little gold snaffles on the instep. His face is permanently choking red.

The Ace Merchant Banker and Lucky Paul have known each other since university, although it wasn't until they met up again in the City that they formed any kind of serious acquaintance. What makes the Ace Merchant Banker different from Lucky Paul is that the Ace Merchant Banker comes from a working-class family. He is a dazzling testimonial to the state education system. He went to a grammar school, on to Cambridge, and then to the City to make some money. His parents don't know what to make of him. He buys them extensions for their house.

He says to Paul, 'I'm leaving the job. I'm giving in my notice on Friday. I can't go on doing this till I croak.'

'What?' Paul coughs.

'I mean, I work from 7.30 a.m., to 7 p.m., sometimes 10 p.m. on long days. I have to call Tokyo at midnight. I get the weekends off, but otherwise, it's work, work, work. Then I get a holiday. Then work, and each time I take a break I'm more tired than the last time.'

Lucky Paul's immediate assumption is that the Ace Mercant Banker is due for some kind of forced retirement. Perhaps he's been found doing a little insider dealing. Some American houses are so wickedly sensitive about insider trading that they build complex regulations around their employees to make sure it doesn't happen. Salomon Brothers, for instance, put a block on anyone dealing in the shares they specialize in.

Maybe he's been caught up in one of those evil little scuffles for position within the firm. But then the Ace Merchant Banker is too good at his job, too straight for either of those to fit.

No, the Ace Merchant Banker's reasons are more diffuse than that. He doesn't like his work enough to go on doing it. 'There are a lot of people who feel this way,' he argues. 'I'm a director. I get paid a lot of money. I have responsibility. I have fun. But my home life ... It's not so bad now, but for the last three years I haven't been to a dinner party where someone hasn't called me from work.'

The Ace Merchant Banker and his girlfriend are the perfect couple for our times. They put in long hours, get paid a lot of money, consume, almost without thinking, televisions and videos, holidays to Thailand, German cars, meals in restaurants, shirts that cost as much as two pairs of trousers, suits that cost the same as a summer holiday. From time to time, the poor people from a nearby council estate wade down to their flat and break into it, stealing the video and the electronic cameras. Still, in material terms, the Ace Merchant Banker and his exactly-groomed girlfriend have the lot. Except that all this comfort starts to be undermined when the office calls him up at 9.30 in the evening in the middle of the main course to consult on an overnight currency transaction.

'The *last* dinner party we went to, I spent half the time on the phone. I mean, they were very decent about it, people usually understand, but ... You know, there are these guys who really stick it out and get to the top, but they don't have any other lives. They're bachelors, or they have marriages that leave them completely independent. You can't do both things. I'm not *that* ambitious. I just think I should be doing something more – socially useful ...' The Ace Merchant Banker stumbles into embarrassed silence. Socially useful. Lucky Paul's radical past suddenly springs into focus as the Ace Merchant Banker says the words.

The grizzled chops are taken away. Lucky Paul and the Ace Merchant Banker both elect for the special bread-and-butter pudding. You can eat all kinds of fancy food in the City these days, denatured *nouvelle cuisine* at *Rouxl Britannia* (where the food comes in a block of ice from the Roux brothers' depot and the only cooking required is the accurate programming of a microwave), saucy little shavings of veal at Corney & Barrow's underground joint in Moorgate, outrageous sandwiches from Birley's (tuna fish, green peppers, Emmental and fresh mayonnaise in one tumultous offering.) You don't have to bloat yourself on mutton or beef. But City people do still like a pudding, a proper, sweet, dense confection. Menus in reconstituted modish bars and *brasseries* will lead you gaily through a programme of little salads and refreshing fish surprises, only to lurch into jam roll and custard at the foot of the page.

'I don't mean social work. What I want to do, is make something, do something with my name on it. Take some money and open a shop maybe. Sell things. I don't know. Run a business.'

Is this something to do with the Ace Merchant Banker's background? Something bred into him about the parasitism of the professions? It is a feeling Lucky Paul frequently gets when he has to tease ideas out of the managing directors and chief executives. That notion that to make is to do; while to think is to waste time.

And there is a strain of repressed entrepreneurial yearning in the City. Many people, brokers, financiers, traders, see their job as a hard cash preface to another life in which they leave the screens and the battery pens, and go off to work at some project only they know about. If everyone with these wordless ambitions actually left the City and set up in business at the same time, it would mean a welter of new wine merchants, antiques dealers, interior design partnerships (with the wife as the creative force), building renovators, restaurateurs, independent film producers, small manufacturing companies which specialize in top-of-the-range lighting equipment, and novelty goods importers. There wouldn't be room in the economy. But the vein is there. The Ace Merchant Banker is one among thousands.

'What's really depressing,' he goes on, 'are these guys who didn't make it, who started to freewheel. People say, he used to be a star, five, six years ago. Now everyone's stepping over him and trying to get him out of the way. I don't want to be in that position ten years from now. Anyway, what's the point of making £150,000 a year if you only ever see your girlfriend for twelve hours at weekends?'

How much exactly is the Ace Merchant Banker *worth*? Paul wonders. There aren't any clear giveaways in the clothes he wears or the accessories he carries with him. By contrast the toff at the next table is buried in an outfit as ruthlessly tribal as anything from Java or New Guinea. There is a sensibility involved in every tuck, pleat, button, pattern, texture. The striped cotton shirt modulates into the spotty silk tie; the suit (both dazzling and funereal) devolves into the rich playfulness of the shoes with their little gold snaffles. The gold ring on the little finger of the left hand suggests luxury, vanity; while the determinedly greasy taming of the hair offers up, in contrast, a kind of self-denial, a refusal to allow the lurking sensuality of hair to get out of hand. Everything is at once restrained and flamboyant, arrogant but unostentatious.

The Ace Merchant Banker, on the other hand, takes a more everyday approach. He wears a suit that could have come from a chainstore, a plain white shirt with none of the detailing of the toff's Jermyn Street purchase, a flat gold watch with the maker's name in midget letters and no obvious trademarks (no Ω, no lumpen Rolex metalwork), and a tie of arresting ordinariness. In fact, he doesn't look like anything or anybody, much. Plenty of folk come into the City with welded shoes, nylon jackets and a Finchley twang in their voices, and by six months have shed it all, reemerging like some booby from the *Tatler and Bystander*. They may subsequently get their sons into hard public schools where they can pick up the habits at first hand. But the Ace Merchant Banker isn't interested in that kind of social engineering. He is, in fact, too confident of himself to bother with dressing-up. That's how much he's worth, Lucky Paul surmises.

The Ace Merchant Banker resigns on Friday. No sooner has he handed over the letter than two other directors take him off for a large meal at Wiltons and press gifts on him till his eyes water. You want a different car? You can have a BMW convertible. You can have a Range Rover. What are you taking home these days? £200,000 after the bonus? Let's bring that up to a quarter of a million. You want to move jobs? You want more travel? You want less travel? You want a different desk – and so on. By the following Tuesday, the Ace Merchant Banker has withdrawn his letter of resignation. He is making still more money. The business venture will have to wait.

The British Airways grand flotation was more of a success than Lucky Paul had anticipated. The amount on offer was £223m. The amount posted by subscribers to the issue, came to £8bn. The event was oversubscribed by thirty-five times. What's more, when the 65p part-paid shares started trading on the 11 February, they were marked straight up to 119½p each, and carried on accumulating value from that point onwards.

Lucky Paul's father couldn't believe it. He got 500 shares and a refund. What was he going to do? If he sold them on the first day of trading, he'd clear a £250.00 profit. If he waited, they might — what? There didn't seem to be any strong reason why they should go *down*. Lucky Paul was for stagging. Lucky Paul's mother, her mind reeling with the prospect of £250 plucked out of the air wanted Paul's father to sell them straight away and buy some new chair covers. But he was so taken with them, and with the token of good fortune that they represented, that he resolved to leave them in the portfolio, waiting for some moment of speculative insight to arrive.

Meanwhile, something had snapped in Paul's mother's head. She'd absorbed random details from her husband's obsessive musings over share issues, portfolio speculation, price projections. She'd registered, a month too late, that British Gas was a gift. And once the British Airways sale had blossomed in front of her eyes, she conceived the maxim that if a thing was sponsored by the Government (for whom she had canvassed mightily in 1983) then it was, if not money in the bank, then money separated from the bank by only the shortest distance. She inspected the sum in her building society account. There was nothing to stop *her* going stagging, when the mood took her, she decided.

5

MARCH: SNOBBERY

One of the stockbrokers involved in the British Airways sell-off was Cazenove & Co. They were also one of the stockbrokers involved in the Guinness-Distillers takeover. They are among the most prominent stockbrokers in the City. And they manage, like Lloyd's, to be preposterous yet, somehow, worth paying attention to. They are a curious firm.

While just about everyone else in the City was busy with surgery in time for the new age and the Big Bang, Cazenoves weren't. They simply 'made provision' to keep themselves liquid. The mysterious investors who put up this money are called 'The Friends Of Caz', like something out of a Baroness Orczy novel. While the conglomerates and multinationals were dying to tell the world how meritocratic, modern, businesslike they were, Cazenoves kept a nagging silence. While boards of directors plunged their firms into tower blocks with *atria* and dealing floors bigger than department stores, Cazenoves impishly stayed put in their Tokenhouse Yard mansion.

They are as aristocratic as it's possible to be, while remaining in some sort of trade. They have a little nobleman's crest (a Hollywood mixture of visors, heraldic beasts and brick castle walls) floating above the 'CAZENOVE' of their writing paper. There are thirty-six listed partners who flank the 'CAZENOVE', and of that thirty-six, no less than eighteen partners' names bear some kind of outright signifier of class. There are the three and four Christian name men (the Hon. V. M. G. A. Lampson; B. M. de L. Cazenove); there are the double-barrels (Wentworth-Stanley; Palmer-Tomkinson; Mitford-Slade); there's even a Lord Faringdon. The senior partner, John Kemp-Welch, comes from a family which occupies a whole page of *Burke's Peerage*. If you had to invent a City firm of toffs and grandees, it would look like Cazenoves. Even the building they inhabit is a reproach to Warburgs' morbid black glass chest or James Capel's chrome greenhouse. Cazenoves live very properly in a clarety Queen Anne-style townhouse down an alley. There are bits of brass attached to the doors. The place is a refutation of the squalidly modern ambitions of the foreigners and the panicky multinationals.

Some see Cazenoves as the last tsars of the City, a firm whose combination of wisdom, authority and sheer snottiness, puts them above all other broking firms. For these people, Cazenoves beat Phillips & Drew, the supersmart James Capel, and the fashionable Warburg Securities (containing the relics of Rowe & Pitman, another grandee stockbrokers). Cazenoves have more clients on their books (according to *Crawford's Directory of City Connections*) than anyone else, with around 250 names. These include Jaguar, Hawker Siddeley, British Telecom, Cable & Wireless and other huge enterprises. Not only that, but they advised the Government when it was selling British Airways, British Gas, BP, British Telecom, anything which had *British* in its name. Others, like Warburgs and James Capel, were involved; but no one was quite as involved as Cazenoves.

The reason for this, supposedly, is that Cazenoves have – or at least had, until their involvement in the Guinness scandal – something called placing power. It is said that when Cazenoves get a bundle of shares they have to sell to the institutional investors and the people with very big money, then they have no difficulty in getting the investors to take the shares off their hands. While other broking houses kill themselves trying to tempt the institutions to take Amalgamated Consolidated Plc, by giving them rich lunches, dynamic presentations, hours of banana-oil down the telephones, Cazenoves inform the buyer in question that he will be *allowed* so many shares in Amalgamated Consolidated Plc and that he should be grateful for the opportunity. And if the intended purchaser of these things says he doesn't need them or want them, then Cazenoves let it be known that he'll be excised from the list of preferred customers when something good next come along. So the investor invests in Cazenoves' offering and Cazenoves gild a little more this certainty that they more than anyone else have placing power. That, at least, is the story. They also, enthusiasts are keen to point out, have all the good things that modern brokers require, like shrewd researchers and a knot of especially thrusting partners to keep the firm racing towards the horizon. But it's placing power that makes them special.

But placing power also means snobbery. Some people are less impressed by Cazenoves' capacity for selling stocks and shares than by the sheer, numbing arrogance their approach reveals. Placing power like this can make you a target for those who subscribe to the principle of a new City, free to all. The ruthlessness of placing power revives notions which many are keen to bury, such as cultism, social ruthlessness, pride. Webb and the Finance King both keep a corner of bile in their hearts for Cazenoves, because Cazenoves embody an attitude which is as much social as professional. Cazenoves attract the kind of resentment which feeds on stories that the shoddier clients have to go up to the partners' floor in the service lift, and that the writing paper is infested with the names of toffs who merit entire pages of *Burke's Peerage*. How can the greater world take the City seriously with this kind of antique revisionism lingering on in Tokenhouse Yard? It's precisely this kind of thing which the City, the meritocrats complain, must lose if it's going to progress.

The Ace Merchant Banker, and plenty of others, will maintain that quite apart from Cazenoves, the City is actually still alive with bigotries and social obsessions. The old division of social possibilities into very smart people and barrow boys no longer hold. Instead there are a hundred ways to rub your sense of self into the faces of others. It's like a polyglot community; although everyone speaks some kind of English, they all have a native tongue which they save for their own kind or to make a point with someone from another race.

Lucky Paul, with his education and his professional-middle-class upbringing, sees the place as robustly mimicking the world outside. There are working-class types (not the Ace Merchant Banker, who has moved into a personal universe where class ceases to exist), lower-middle classers, toffs and suburbanites dotted around the streets and buildings. There are LIFFE traders, dealers, office messengers and gofers, boys from Hoxton who wear armoured loafers, white socks and suits that are tailored with garden shears. There are quietly unformidable thinkers and workers, with unpretentious homes. There are all kinds in the City, and they all get along together somehow. That's what Lucky Paul comfortably asserts. But he overlooks the truth.

For instance, you may be a pension fund manager whose pension fund is worth billions, but you are still a strictly meat-and-potatoes guy. You are invited to lunch with a grandee stockbroking firm in one of their famous panelled dining rooms (you may, equally be a meat-and-potatoes Finance King, shuffling into the home of a grandee bank). The nicest grandee stockbroker in the world pours you a drink, discusses the view from the window, murmurs confidentialities in your ear. Your suit is partly wool, partly polyester. It keeps its shape marginally better than a supermarket bag. His suit is all wool, and laps his pleasurably overfed body like a great blue glove. He wears the golden signet ring of class on his finger. He says, 'absolutely', and 'orf', and 'quite appalling'. He has a way of smiling at you from some kind of vantage point within his head: *I'm smiling*, he seems to say, *but I want you to think of it as purely decorative.* His warm, modulated drawl comes from a set of vocal chords that were made by an expert, while yours were made by a machine. You have a pile of money under your control, you are here, legitimately, in this grandee room, the stockbroker is being conspicuously sweet to you, but how could you ever buy a voice like his?

Or try this: in a bar at lunchtime, you (a meat-and-potatoes kind of guy) are lodged in the musty pack of suits struggling to get their orders across the counter. A bottle of Sancerre and two glasses! Three red wines! Two Becks, a Perrier and a bottle of Muscadet. You feel a tap on your shoulder. You turn round to face some rangy boy, perhaps twenty-five years old, his face mottled with drinking. He says, plummily, 'Do you know the way to Paxman Street?' You think. Paxman Street? Who *is* this person? You stumble out a 'no', with as much of a helpless nice-guy shrug as you can manage in the press. He says, 'Well, fucking well learn', and vanishes into the street outside.

Or this. Three City yobs are standing outside an investment bank's front door. They know each other. They wear armoured loafers and sack suits. They sport little chains (gold, silver) around the wrist and throat. They say, 'bollocks', and 'cunt'. They jab each other in the ribs. Two of them reel away to a parked red Ferrari. The third disappears back into the investment bank. The Ferrari driver fires the engine, bangs it into first gear and heads straight for the meat-and-potatoes guy's knees as he starts to cross the road. He hears the car coming, sees it, falls back against a little, aged, office gofer in a blue mac, and the blissful yobs in the Ferrari speed towards the Commercial Road.

Like the gilded stockbroker, you can be arrogant by birth and upbringing. Anyone who goes through a genuine public school gets their parents' money's worth. Tough, rich schools are still turning out products who are vigorously, shamelessly snotty. Even those who worry about their snottiness (Lucky Paul, again) can't shed it. It's something that denotes who you are, as much as the colour of your skin or the shape of your nose.

Or you can learn to be a snob when you go to university. Oxford and Cambridge have a lot to answer for, here. A grammar school product who gets a scholarship to King's can learn how to be breathtakingly unpleasant in his three tumultuous years there. And if you dislike someone principally because you find them common, but educated scruple forbids you to name that as your reason for doing so, then you can always belittle them by saying that *they just haven't got it*, and tapping your temple with a dismissive Forefinger.

Or you can buy it. Your money gives you the chance to live out dreams of class envy and snob hatred, becoming, in the process, a monster of cash-rich arrogance yourself.

And what happens to the meat-and-potatoes guy? He bottles it all up until he's in the company of more meat-and-potatoes guys (fund managers for insurance companies; the staff of the smaller stockbroking firms, maybe, and looses his tongue on the toffs and the yobs with their voices and their cars. And all the meat-and-potatoes guys nod, and say, 'They give the place a bad name,' and, 'the newspapers love all that kind of thing,' and, 'they're as bad as each other.'

The younger yobs and toffs *are* as bad as each other. They address one another in an eerily consonant, bullying way which comes either from Big School in between lessons, or from ravaged youth clubs and underage pubs. And why not? They have a lot to get off their chests. They get tense, they get aggressive. They grab each other's ties, and say, Is that real silk? Shall I show you if it's real silk or not? (No! No! It's silk! Let go!) I'll just stick my lighted cigar into it . . . (Christ! Fuck off!) There you are. Didn't burn. Real silk . . .

When they want to persuade a party to join them in a restaurant (a bar, a club, a showing of Arnold Schwarzenegger in *Predator*) they say, For fuck's sake, don't be a *wimp*! You're wimping out! Come *on*, you bastard! Finish that fucking drink and come *on*! When there are women present (this excludes airheaded secretaries and office gofers, whom they might want to impress, or at least, get into bed) then the women can either shut up or bark as loud as the men. They do it outside the City. Go to a party in a Fulham maisonette and who are the City workers but the ones prodding each other hard in the short ribs and radiating a kind of neurotic raucousness . . . God! That's *pathetic* . . . He asked me if I'd drive his bloody Range Rover back from France for him . . . I said, don't be fucking stupid, do it yourself . . . What a purler! Couldn't get off the floor . . .

Then, when you come back to Cazenoves, they take you out of the polyglot City, and back thirty years. Not only does senior partner John Kemp-Welch merit *Burke's Peerage*, he was also 'brought to the front door' of the firm. In other words, his father, a partner at Cazenoves before him, took advantage of their unwritten law which permits partners to introduce a son into the business, by right. This is unregenerate nineteenth-century privilege. What happened to the new age? What about the meritocracy? The Cazenoves' reply is that the privilege of bringing a son to the front door comes with a latter-day countercheck. Cazenoves have to perform like anyone else. Anyone who manages to escape the process of selection at the start, has to prove themselves by working harder once they're in. This is Cazenoves' riposte. But what sticks in your mind is the privilege, not the drawbacks that cling to it. In the same way, the fact that Henry de Lerisson Cazenove is a Grand Director of Ceremonies in the Supreme Council of the 33rd Degree – that is to say, an important and industrious Freemason – encourages you to think of Cazenoves as a place where social connections still carry weight.

Does this happen anywhere else in quite the same way? In white goods manufacture (these people make a perfectly good washing machine, but if you want something a little less *parvenu*...); in television companies (I've always found Anglia a very pleasant company to work with; small, but extremely well-connected...); in fertilisers (they send their stuff round in a velvet bag, and I think it makes things grow that much faster...)? You can guess at two futures for Cazenoves. One is based on the premise that social smartness always sees you through. This is, to some extent, a broader application of a rule that usually applies to individuals – Remember The Hon. Thomas Jaster Manners (educ. Eton) of Lazards? Remember John Chippendale Lindley (Chips) Keswick (educ. Eton) of Hambros? They're in the places that count. Someone has to be at the top, and it's not going to be Webb, in front of his TV screen, or the breweries analyst in the cubicle nest to Lucky Paul, with his telescopic umbrella and his habit of blowing his nose on a paper tissue. Class counts. The same goes for Cazenoves.

The alternative, is that it doesn't; and that the polyglot City, despite its furious internal social divisions, becomes the normal way of doing things. You take on anyone, from anywhere. Cazenoves get smaller and more specialized and more and more perfect and no less aristocratic, until one day they are so small and specialized and perfect and aristocratic that one of the high street clearing banks decides that Cavenoves will fit neatly into half a floor of its chrome and steel head offices, and buys them up.

SOMETHING WENT WRONG AT GREENWELL MONTAGU

Then the FOOTSIE went through 2000 for the first time in its life.

It happened on 4 March 1987, when the index lurched up to 2021.5. By the end of the week it had fallen back to 1998.2, but the feeling was still bullish. Everyone was busy. Since Big Bang, the average daily turnover of the Stock Exchange had swollen like a fat river. In terms of the number of bargains traded, 85 per cent were in domestic equities, worth about £1.1bn per day. A year ago, it had been closer to £600m's worth every day. Gilts were standing at an average daily turnover of around £2.5bn. Foreign equities were doing about £510m a day – up 70 per cent on the previous year. The market makers were hard at work, not just keeping up with trading, but in calculating their commissions. Large purchasers or sellers of shares could expect to pay maybe 0.2 per cent or 0.3 per cent on a deal. Or could they? The *Investor's Chronicle* argued that the total amount of commission paid to brokers was now 60 per cent lower than before Big Bang, and that this wasn't simply the result of bargain rates and slashed prices, but the result of no prices at all. The market makers weren't charging any commissions on deals, but were living off what's known as the touch – the difference between what they pay for a share, and what they sell it for. This no-cost trading, said the *Investor's Chronicle*, took up about half the total market.

Now, this is all right in a bull market, since the sheer mass of turnover will keep the £100m outfits going, provided their market makers don't go heavily into the wrong stocks, or somehow miss out in the general demand for shares. But two things spring to mind. What happens if the market turns down, and no one wants to buy? And what happens if your dealing floor doesn't make the right deals? The first question is one of those fidgety imponderables that really is its own answer. If things go wrong, we all suffer, is about the best anyone could say to it. As for the second, Midland Montagu produced an answer on 13 March, when it told the world that it was closing the market-making department of Greenwell Montagu Securities.

Greenwell Montagu was the fairly typical product of a Big Bang chaos of ambitions. The Midland Bank, like its three big high street colleagues, had decided to make a showing in the deregulated City. Lloyds Bank did it by spontaneously generating a virgin stock-broking department to add to their merchant banking division. The others did it by consuming living firms. Barclays ate up stockbrokers de Zoete & Bevan, and old-time jobbers, Wedd Durlacher Mordaunt. The National Westminster paid for Fielding Newson-Smith and Bisgood Bishop. The Midland got Samuel Montagu, the bankers, and two brokers – Smith Keen Cutler, and W. Greenwell, a broking outfit which was held to be up with the Hoare Govetts and the

Grieveson Grants, even the grandee Cazenoves. But the Midland Bank is, if not accident-prone, at least not as breezily dynamic as NatWest or Barclays. It spent quite a lot of time and money in the 1980s getting badly entangled with an American bank called Crocker, in which it had taken a share and into which it threw more and more money before finally selling off the broken remnants in 1986. In the late 1940s, it had been the world's biggest bank. Now, it was the smallest of the big four UK high street banks. It had also shackled itself with a promotional campaign centred around a cartoon griffin which popped out, smirking, at customers when they came in to get their cash. On this count alone, the Midland was not a serious bank.

When Midland's head office worked out that Greenwell Montagu was posting a £6m loss on the market-making side, they simply axed the thing. Unlike Barclays or NatWest, the Midland had no kind of impossible wealth to abandon to this tyro City enterprise. At the beginning of the year, Barclays had cheerlessly poured £160m into BZW, to sustain its operations. But not the Midland. Some people were sacked. Some senior market makers packed themselves off to Scrimgeour Vickers. It was a gasp of cold air (like Geoffrey Collier; like Guinness) in the jungly heat of the bull market and the *Annus Mirabilis*. You *could* make mistakes. You *could* go wrong. Not everyone was going to last the course. One estimate suggested that the total loss to the Midland bank, including all the money it had taken to start the outfit up, came to over £40m. And this was when things were going as well as they possibly could go.

There was something else, a veiled current of thought, a remark that almost wasn't there but which people picked up all the same: Greenwell Montagu screwed up, because the parent company was *common*. The Midland Bank, not only a high street clearing bank but the smallest high street clearing bank, and a bank with a cartoon griffin as its corporate symbol, the Midland Bank just wasn't right for the City. It was slightly – vulgar – shabby. They shouldn't have meddled in a culture they couldn't understand. Greenwells were a perfectly proper outfit. They were the right sort. Now look at them. That's what happens if you get involved with the wrong sort.

There are also some City activities that proper City people don't do. There is business going on in the new polyglot community which is very tricky and risky business. There is a parallel world to the everyday of gilts, equities, commodities, a realm of trading which trades on other trades; which speculates on speculation; which second-guesses itself. This is the world of Futures and Options. It is a world for the real finance junkie.

It is also doing well. Take traded options in UK equities: by mid-1987, this was running at around 50,000 contracts a day, up 180 per cent on the previous year. On the London International Financial Futures Exchange, trading volume loitered at around 4000 bargains a day in 1983, but by 1987 was averaging 54,583 daily bargains. The traded options market generally is growing at around 9 per cent per month, on a compound basis. The financial futures market is arguably the fastest growing area in the financial world. LIFFE handles financial futures and financial options; the Stock Exchange does equities and currency options; the London Commodity Exchange deals with commodity futures contracts (cocoa, coffee, oil products, things you can in theory pick up and *feel*); the London Metal Exchange handles hard commodity contracts; the Baltic Exchange deals with commodity and shipping freight futures on its Baltic International Freight Futures Exchange (watch out for BIFFEX, the goofiest acronym in the City); the London Foreign Exchange Market does forward currency contracts. You can't avoid these things, these finance junkie's toys.

Wait, say the people who run them; they're not toys. They're not gimmicks. Take options and futures. These are similar, but not quite the same. A futures contract gives its buyer the right to purchase a commodity (or a bundle of money) at a particular date in the future, for a certain price. An option gives the buyer the option, but not the obligation, to buy or sell a commodity (a bundle of money, a bundle of shares) for a certain price, up to a certain date in the future. These are useful financial products, which serve a consumer need, and make the world a better place.

This is how: take a bedrock futures contract, say an interest rate futures bargain. Suppose a corporate treasurer, a Finance King, knows that he'll have to borrow £1m for a period of three months, in three months' time. Interest rates *now* are 10 per cent. He does nothing. Three months go by, he borrows the money. But interest rates have gone up to 12 per cent, so he pays more for his £1m than if he'd been able to borrow when interest rates were lower (this is maybe, *your* company, *your* job). His notional loss is £5000. But suppose the Finance King is wise to futures contracts. This time, he sells four contracts on LIFFE *now*, each for £250,000, at 90. He has to put down a deposit of £6000, as does the buyer of the contracts. Interest rates go up 2 per cent, the price of sterling futures goes down to 88, the buyer is still in with a contract at 90, the seller (the Finance King) makes a profit of £5000, which exactly meets the extra cost of borrowing, when the borrowing happens at 12 per cent. The punter who *bought* the contract, loses £5000. The buyer and seller never get round to exchanging £1m. That's not the point. They close out the position before the contract expires, as is the case with most financial futures contracts.

On the options market, the Finance King might buy an option to borrow £1m at 10 per cent interest in three months' time. The option seller sells him this option and charges an upfront fee of 1 per cent (10 per cent on £1m for three months is £25,000. The seller takes a tenth of this, in other words £2500 for his pains). Well, interest rates go up to 12 per cent, and the Finance King exercises his option to borrow at 10 per cent. If he'd borrowed at the going rate for three months, his borrowing costs would be £30,000. Because he's wise to options, his costs are only £25,000 — although he has to add on to that the £2500 he paid for the option, so that the total saving is only £2500. But then, £2500 in the bank is better than £2500 out of the bank.

Now these examples suggest that futures and options are good things, because they help the Finance King avoid the risk of getting punished by a move in interest rates. He pays a premium, he gets some insurance. If interest rates had gone *down* while he'd had his futures contract out at 10 per cent, he'd have lost his premium; but then his borrowing costs would have been lower. You pay for prudence.

But you can also use your options to speculate. This gets some people, the finance junkies, as well as the risk-containers, into a sweat of anticipation. Suppose you are sitting on some Amalgamated Consolidated Plc shares, and they are worth 250p. You are bored with them. You think that the price may go down in the next few months. You write an option to sell your shares (called a 'put' option) for 250p at any time until the end of the next quarter. Some other punter thinks the share price will go up, not down. He buys the option for the little premium of 15p that you ask. If the price goes up to 270p, the punter exercises his right to buy at 250p, and still gets the shares for 5p a share less than he'd pay in the market. If the price does nothing much, or goes down, then you keep the shares (or even sell them once the option's expired) and you also keep the other punter's premium.

Better still, you start trading the options themselves. Forget the shares! Who needs the shares? If you buy an option to purchase some Amalgamated Consolidated shares at 250p (this is known as a 'call' option) for 15p, you can then sell your option to another speculator for, perhaps 20p if it looks as if Amalgamated Consolidated shares are going to increase their price. The buyer of your call option might then sell that on for 25p to a third speculator, if the underlying share price continues to look healthy. Perhaps the option changes hands five times, and hits a maximum price of 60p, while Amalgamated Consolidated rises to 300p. The gain on the original option price is merely 40p. But if you express this gain as a percentage growth, then it works out at 200 per cent. The shares which generate this gain, have gone up by 50p, but then that's only a 20 per cent gain on the initial share price. The option becomes a speculator's dream invention. If you bought a minimum traded options contract (which would embrace 1000 Amalgamated Consolidated shares) for 20p a share, you'd have to pay £200. But if you held on to your options until the moment at which they were worth 60p, as a result of all the busy trading going on, you'd get back £600 and make a clear £400 profit. It's hard to conceive of another investment which could pay you a return at that rate, in an equally short space of time – maybe no more than a few months. The figures suggest that around 3000 transactions take place every day, with an average of nineteen contracts making up each trans-action. At the moment, this magical generation of a large price change as the result of a small price change (the kind of alchemical contingency that the City loves) is only held back by the types of company in which you can trade options. There are about sixty quoted on the Stock Exchange, and they're all blue-chip, big-time, unshocking businesses like ICI and Shell. If they start trading options in the smaller high-risk, huge-rewards-and-cataclysmic-losses companies, then the market will become a chaotic brothel of money desires.

The obverse of all this, is that if you buy a call option for 50p and the price of Amalgamated Consolidated abruptly sticks, or goes down, then your option is going to lose its worth at the same exponential rates. It might just die in your hand if the option expires before Amalgamated Consolidated shares pick up, or give the im-pression of being about to pick up. The same fundamental problem exists for the futures trader. If the price of the currency or com-modity moves against you, and you're lumbered with the contract when the time comes for your opposite number to collect, then you *lose*. You don't suffer a spasm of horror, followed by the kind of morbid portfolio reshuffling a fund manager or an individual equities investor would undergo. They can mix things up and then wait for them to improve with time. But if your futures or options contract expires, then you close out, and have to start again with another gamble on another day. You *lose* that sum of money.

Whatever their apologists say, there's something about this kind of trading that arouses irrational feelings. You can see that it has a function that's as necessary and useful as anything else that goes on in the City. Nothing happens there which doesn't owe its being to a genuine market demand. But at the same time, it provokes an uneasy kind of mental groping: something (you find yourself thinking) has to be wrong here. The speculation's all at one remove. You're not putting your money on a share, and hoping that its price will go up; you're putting your money on the movement itself, on the financial spirit of the share, its monetary ghost. Gilts and equities are signs of the real world. You hold shares in a company that has an existence. When you enter into a futures contract, you're buying into a price, not a thing. When you write an option on a currency, you're taking a view on a row of numbers. The numbers you use to get into the contract are the substance of the contract itself. The single most actively traded option isn't even an equity option – although British Telecom, Rolls Royce, GEC are all popular – its most actively traded option is based on the FOOTSIE, the Stock Exchange Index. Around 6000 FOOTSIE options are traded every day. They account for 13 per cent of the options market. Things have acquired a metaphysical status. Everything is abstract. People will trade an interest in a number, before they trade an interest in a company.

Maybe this is why LIFFE, the London International Financial Futures Exchange, gets so much attention. Caryl Churchill's play *Serious Money* is set on the floor of LIFFE. The *Sunday Times Magazine* ran a cover story on a LIFFE trader called David Kyte. They photographed him standing grouchily outside the Royal Exchange building (in which LIFFE is housed) and hollered, 'On a good day the man on the left makes £100,000.' It turned out that this was the trading profit for his particular firm, rather than his take-home pay. Money like this, as the Ace Merchant Banker will tell you, is actually nothing special. But there he was, filling in the one day of the week when *Serious Money* wasn't on.

Much of LIFFE's appeal comes from its manners and habits, as well as from the ontological qualms it produces. Now that the Stock Exchange floor is dead, we need a place where we may watch the physical excitement of deals and money being made. The Metal Exchange (another exchange that involves shouting and waving) is too small, and the Baltic Exchange, where brokers amble about between pillars of marble, feels like a Spa at the end of the season. But LIFFE (blessed with the trashy pun of its own name) is a party.

The dealing system in LIFFE is called 'open outcry'. Traders stand in and on the perimeter of a shallow grave called a 'pit'. They shout at each other, trying to match bargains. They wave their arms. They make cabbalistic signs with their hands (the palm faces away from the body, the trader wants to sell contracts; the palm faces towards the body, the trader wants to buy contracts; the number of fingers held up, with the hand near to the body, shows the number of contracts to be traded). They wear coloured blazers, like sportsmen, some blue, some yellow and white, some red, to indicate which firms they're trading for. The man Kyte and his assistants wear red white and blue with an enormous 'KYTE' stamped on the back. It's a pageant. It's mediaeval. The traders yell across the pit, toss chits through the air to their booths, shred paper into confetti and throw it up high, rag each other, jostle, twitch, fidget, bark, stamp around. All these boys and girls, the brilliant crowd . . . Caryl Churchill sensibly milked it for its stage visuals. There is no difference between the syncopated hysterics of *Serious Money* and LIFFE, except that LIFFE is bigger and more hysterical. We applaud its vulgarity and energy.

But what are they trading? A chasm opens up between the hard-nut reality of the institution, and the invisible business that drives it on. David Kyte is flesh and blood. He wears his Union Jack blazer and yanks open his collar and scrags his tie and makes things happen in the pit. You catch sight of him, and you think, there's Kyte, the man who was in the *Sunday Times* Magazine. A real person; you know all about him from the article. But what sustained the piece, what gave it its reason for being, and what makes Kyte so obscurely interesting, is the idea that he does something which has no meaning in our world. In the article, he was annoyed because he'd gone wrong on some US bonds. Instead of making £1.25m, he'd lost £63,000. That kind of thing happens all the time in the City. The thing that made Kyte's bad news more savoury for the gently boggling reader was the underlying certainty that he was trying to make money from a purely imaginary trade, a trade in hunches, guesswork, feelings, anticipated numbers. He was the incarnation of the City's need to conjure money from nothing. In a moment of real bewilderment, you might have transfigured David Kyte into Joseph Knecht, *Magister Ludi* of *The Glass Bead Game*, the Herman Hesse invention which synthesizes cultural realities into a game of essential, inner abstractness.

That's one reason why LIFFE is a convenient stepping-off point for the main story of *Serious Money*; not just because it presents a piece of folkloric City anarchy, but because the people in LIFFE make money out of pure abstractions. So the shift into the real business of the play (invisible insider trading and the organized fictions of a takeover bid) is a natural one.

*

There's something else too. There's the question of propriety; the question of gambling. From one angle, futures and options are clearly ways of limiting your exposure to unpleasant events. You can buy yourself insurance to cover your currency needs, your import bills, downturns in shipping business, share price fluctuations. But insurance, especially this kind of insurance, involves two types of players – the nervous insurer who wants to button things down, and the speculator who takes up the risk in return for money. The City text books habitually describe futures and options as devices for hedging your commitments, for managing your risks. This is where we came in.

But remember the punter who bought the Finance King's futures contracts from him? He made a clear £5000 loss, while the Finance King came out ahead of the game. Where does the punter come from? What's he doing there? In Chicago, where the whole business of futures originated, these speculators are called 'locals', and they hang around the futures markets, providing liquidity and putting their cash up as counterparties to the various deals being struck. Futures started in the nineteenth century, as a way of hedging against price changes in pork bellies. Then people started to trade the futures as hard as they traded the bellies themselves. Then, in 1972, the Chicagoans (the grandsons of the pork bellies men) invented Financial Futures after the Bretton Woods currency agreement fell to pieces and the world's currencies became volatile. It makes sense that Chicago should be the home of these things. Chicagoan grit, wind, hard streets, coin-slot mouths and crushed vowels, all give a kind of mythical colour to the truths of futures speculation. The locals are tough men. They put up thousands and thousands of dollars every day, working the market, checking the books, aiming to come out ahead.

There are locals in London too. Some of them work as intermediaries for other clients; some, like Kyte, are in business for themselves. The rest of the market is carved up by big firms like Merrill Lynch, trading on behalf of their clients. Similarly, the options market is a mixture of stockbroking firms, who use options to contain their exposure to equities movements, investment institutions who do the same, and private clients. You ask a putty-faced options dealer, roped to his screen in the torrid battery pen, who these people *are*, these money-providers, these risk takers, and once he's finished explaining the symbiosis of options and share prices (frantically shuffling his charts, the pretty, graphic coincidences of decline and growth) he says, well, they're just – individuals. People who like to take a position. Rich individuals? They've got money – enough to participate.

That's the other thing about LIFFE, the thing that fixes it in our minds, and which puts it in another corner of City society. There are pure gamblers in these markets, and gamblers don't need to be socially smart. There are two people involved in every deal: one wants the numbers to go up; the other wants them to go down. They put their money in the pot at the beginning, and check the progress of the game. Maybe they decide to sell out before the game finishes, and take the winnings they can, passing the bet on to another player. But there are still two players, one betting on one outcome, one on another. Now anyone who invests in gilts or equities is also a gambler in that he has no guarantee of a return on his investment. He may lose his shirt, but he's playing against something impersonal, not another player. When the market maker sells on a batch of shares to an investor, the deal's over for him. But futures and options players are locked in with each other. It's your estimate against mine. If *you* lose, then necessarily, *I* win.

This nakedness would be too much for Cazenoves. But LIFFE has generated its own clique of boys from the suburbs and the estates. There are new, quick-fire, arcade-game ways of making it in the City. Trading options, trading futures, these are the latest and edgiest games. 'It's not *Oxbridge* in here, it's Uxbridge,' coined the LIFFE floor manager, deliriously. Within a few streets of each other, there are the delicious probities (saving Guinness, of course) of Cazenoves and their seigneurial placing power; and there are the hot, barking pits of LIFFE, packed out with the Hoxton boys in their armoured loafers. The LIFFE trader spurns the grandee – too snotty, too slow, too old-fashioned; and the grandee looks at the LIFFE trader and crosses the street, shuddering inside his blue glove of a suit. And the tedious analyst from a provincial university unfurls his telescopic umbrella as he steps out of his office, in case of rain.

6

SPRING 1987: THE LAW

The Budget came and went in mid-March. The City, in that it had a view of things at all, liked the Budget, mainly because it took 2p off income tax and announced a reduction of the planned Public Sector Borrowing Requirement from £7m to £4m. The Chancellor of the Exchequer dilated on the themes of the collapse in world oil prices, growth in output ('Our growth rate has been the highest of all the major European economies . . .'), inflation ('Over the lifetime of this Parliament, inflation has averaged less than five per cent . . .'), and rounded off with the blithe *Nunc Dimittis* that 'This is a Budget built on success, and a Budget for success.' Neil Kinnock said it was a 'bribes budget', which had 'little to do with the general good and everything to do with the General Election'.

Who cared about the leader of the Opposition? The Labour Party claimed to know nothing about the City except that it was a sink of double-dealing. The money the City earned for the country overall wasn't authentic money. Only money that came from manufacturing, from serious endeavours, was money. That was the philosophy that Labour exuded. So the City turned its back on the Labour Party and thought instead of the sluggish parade of popular opinion polls which had the Conservatives anything from three points to twelve ahead of their Opposition.

But one or two City folk also felt a prickle of apprehension at Chancellor Lawson's little Budget acknowledgement of the rest of the world. 'Given the continuation of present policies in this country,' he said, 'the biggest risk to the excellent prospect I have outlined is that of a downturn in the world economy as a whole. There are still serious imbalances afflicting the three major economies – the USA, Japan and Germany – which, if not handled properly, could lead to a simultaneous downturn in all three.'

The United States was by now looking like a stage glutton, pigging itself on a flood of delicious morsels from the rest of the world. By the end of 1986, it had a $59bn trade deficit running with Japan, and a $16bn trade deficit with West Germany. It also had trade deficits with Taiwan, Korea, Great Britain, Canada and even Mexico. It had a budget deficit of more than $200bn. It was vain-gloriously allowing itself to be legged over by the rest of the world. The rest of the world needed the States to behave like this, of course, so that they could enjoy the fruits of their own hard work. But the gorged wreck was going to make things difficult. And a couple of weeks after the Budget, Japan gestured hilariously in the Great Glutton's face, when the Tokyo Stock Exchange overtook Wall Street for the first time: it showed a value of around $2661bn against Wall Street's $2652bn.

In the same week, there was a small crash in share prices. The FOOTSIE fell 46.1 on Monday, 30 March. On the same day, the older and smaller Financial Times 30-Share Index marked down its biggest ever one-day fall, losing 38.4 points in nine hours. By the end of the week, the FOOTSIE was off by 83.9 points, closing on Friday at 1965.1. What was it? A reassessment? A pause for breath before the next slavering assault on the 2000 and beyond regions of the Index? The start of a slump? Analysts like Lucky Paul fumbled for answers. They came up with an assortment: it was a market revaluation; it was to do with fears about the US economy; the peak of the bull market, as indicated by historical precedent, had formally arrived; it was to do with fears of a trade war between the Americans and the Japanese.

Then nothing happened. The market stretched, shook itself and ran, barking, after the next share price rises. In a couple of weeks, it was going to be right back through 2000, and heading for 2200. Besides, there were things to look forward to. On 18 March the Government had announced yet another vast sell off; this time, it was to be the Government's remaining shares in BP. Once they had got rid of British Gas, with its huge size and its goal of broadening popular capitalism, and British Airways, with all its drawbacks and inadequacies, they were bold enough to release around £7bn of holdings on to a market which already had a price for existing BP shares. The market also knew about oil companies and the world oil markets and their habit of falling flat from time to time. But you still had to make money on it. You still had to go for BP.

And to make the City person's happiness complete, *Serious Money* had opened on the 27 March, at the Royal Court. Irving Wardle, in *The Times*, liked it. He called it 'An angry, witty, front-line report on Britain ... It is a play on the manifold faces of greed ... The face sometimes becomes wholly repellent ... As one character observes, "There's ugly greed; and there's sexy greed — which is the late 1980s" ...' *Serious Money* abused the City with a scalding tongue; it said the City was venal, myopic, incontinent, immoral, gross, brutal, fatuous, criminal, anti-social, vulgar, foul-mouthed and bigoted. As soon as the notices appeared, it sold out to boggling crowds of City people. They loved it.

GUINNESS AND THE SWAMP OF MORALITY

The men from the Fraud Squad arrested Ernest Saunders on Wednesday, 6 May. It happened like this: Saunders, the self-deposed ex-Chairman of Guinness, had been helping the Department of Trade and Industry with its enquiries into the matter of share price manipulation at the time of the Distillers takeover. When the DTI conducts one of its periodic examinations, it usually sets two clean professionals on the case (in this case, a chartered accountant from Peat Marwick McLintock called Ian Watt, and a QC called David Donaldson). The professionals are paid their normal daily rate, interrogate witnesses and go through any documentation of interest, then write a long report. On that Wednesday, Saunders had spent the afternoon discussing things with Watt and Donaldson. He then went on to his solicitors, a firm with the cheerfully seaside name of Payne Hicks Beach.

Saunders was talking with his lawyer, when in came a couple of police officers. They took him off to Holborn police station and charged him with conspiring to pervert the course of justice and destroying company documents. Watt and Donaldson knew nothing about this until it was all over.

The Guinness affair was opening up canyons of suspicion. It was set to be the worst City embarrassment for a decade. The Opposition was calling for an interim report from the DTI straight away, to satisfy public concern. And a member of the Cabinet had allowed the press to know that the Tories were politically exposed (and this with a general election looming before them) until 'We can get the handcuffs on.' Rich Corrupt City types had, over the past year, become cheerfully deplored archetypes, like The Insolent Black or The Giggling Homosexual. We even felt that we knew them better than they knew themselves, after an extensive diet of lid-lifting tabloid stories and quizzical colour features in the broadsheets. There was, it seemed, our world, which subscribed loosely to certain proprieties; and the City world which was as reputable as a firm of loan sharks.

In the City itself, the schism expressed itself like this: you could either be for Saunders or against him. You could extend a tolerant sympathy towards the hard-working executives and specialists (like Saunders, like Seelig) or you could repudiate them. And now you could be working either for the DTI or the Fraud Squad.

DTI investigations have the mustiness of the past clinging to them. They're organized in a way that reflects other values, forgotten precepts. They're not like criminal investigations – more like public inquiries with an ingredient of moralizing thrown in. The DTI published some *Notes For The Guidance Of Inspectors Appointed Under The Companies Act, 1985* – in other words, people like Watt and Donaldson. In the *Notes* the DTI avuncularly cautions its inspectors to 'exercise great restraint when making critical comment . . .' They should 'only do so to the extent unavoidable for the purpose of their reports'. Now, does this sound like apt behaviour in the treatment of suspects? Or in the treatment of people whose business it might be to obscure, rewrite, hide, delete and encumber the evidence of their pasts? What makes it worse (critics of the DTI method argue) is that its inspectors start their inquiries with powers that the police can only dream of. They can require witnesses to appear before them; they can compel these witnesses to speak; they can order documents to be shown to them. They could, if they wanted to, give suspects an appalling time.

But they don't. In 1986, the DTI ran 130 internal company inquiries. These led to thirty-three company winding-up orders and only fifteen successful prosecutions. The DTI also handles insider dealing cases, which the Stock Exchange surveillance unit passes on to them. In 1986, the Stock Exchange alerted the DTI to around a hundred suspected insider dealings, but the DTI declined to investigate more than three of them. Not only that, but the DTI's inquiries can last forever. Of the fifteen company investigations going on at the time of Saunders' arrest in 1987, seven had been going on for more than *three years*. Some of the suspects involved had simply fled to another part of the world.

It leaves the DTI investigators in an ambiguous position, and with a kind of truncated authority, one which can generate a shiver of unpleasantness but which then disappears in a mist of interviews and drudge-like fact-finding.

Along with the general upturn in City business, there was also a small boom in DTI investigations. By May 1987, the DTI found itself in the most exciting professional circumstances. There were company investigations into Consolidated Goldfields, House of Fraser Holdings and, of course, Guinness. There were insider trading investigations into the hapless Morgan Grenfell (Collier's purler, which was at least straightforward, given the man's blow-by-blow confession), the British and Commonwealth shipping and finance group, and into the DTI itself.

This last was the result of a particularly diligent piece of newspaper reporting. It had turned out that there was a mole within the DTI who was passing on information about Monopolies Commission referrals. Sometimes a takeover bid which is running smoothly to form ends up before the Monopolies and Mergers Commission on suspicion of prejudicing the public interest. An MMC referral can come right out of the sky. It blocks the takeover, the investors get depressed, and the shares of the target company, which have increased in value as the bidder tries to buy them up, collapse. This had happened with Norton Opax's bid for the McCorquodale printing firm, and with Hillsdown Holdings' bid for S. & W. Berisford. What had also happened was that a ring of investors had sold the target company's shares just before the MMC referral came out. It had happened too often to be prescience. Someone was letting them in on the DTI's plans. So the

DTI set a pair of experts on the case.

But were they going to give the villains, if they ever found them, the treatment they deserved? Or were they going to exercise restraint when making a critical comment? The Director of Public Prosecutions clearly thought that Guinness was a bad thing, but that the DTI would approach it too punctiliously. So he put the Fraud Squad on to Saunders, and they arrested him instead. Attitudes were changing. It was time for decisive moves, preempting all the tiresome report writing and evidence sifting. Things were getting nastier, and the Civil Service traditions which inform the DTI's way of doing things were looking more and more irrelevant.

There was a curious adjunct to this change in state procedure. The Fraud Squad became popular. Now the police, in particular, the Metropolitan Police, spend a lot of time trying to fend off the opprobrium of the rest of society. It gets harder every day to find anyone who'll unequivocally endorse a policeman. But as Guinness started to develop, the Fraud Squad officers evolved into oddly charismatic lead players. The *Evening Standard* ran a profile of the two men leading the Fraud Squad investigation. The tone of the piece was uncritically awed. 'Detective Superintendent Richard Botwright,' it began, 'the man in charge of the Metropolitan Police Fraud Squad's inquiry into the affairs of Guinness Plc, stands 6ft 2in, is well-built, has large hands and frankly, looks more like one of those much-too-handsome TV cops than a guy who's now spent 25 years wearing a badge and arresting real-life murderers.' Later on, we hear that 'Botwright moves in close, sure of himself and shows he isn't one to give anything away. "Who are you?" "A guy who's here to meet someone." "Who would that be?" "I thought it was you." "Depends on who you are." Funny, but when you run up against a guy that big who's worn a badge for 25 years, the Dashiell Hammett dialogue rings true . . .'

Botwright's colleague, Detective Chief Inspector John Wootton, doesn't enjoy such a eulogy. He, it turns out, has 'A squarish face, big shoulders and a loose-fitting raincoat. At first glance, it appears as if Central Casting has sent over a really tough guy to play sidekick . . .' Still, he shares Botwright's ravishing limelight.

It goes on. 'When you're playing poker at these stakes, you never show more of your own hand than you have to ... interviews are conducted with practiced *politesse* and with an accent on courtesy ... although the interviewers are definitely firm in their obviously determined approach ...' This goes against the grain. For years, the Mets have been whipping-boys, stooges, thugs. Even right-wing papers like the *Standard* appreciate the mileage in a Bent Copper story, while a populist TV show like *Minder* takes it as an axiom that the police are more venal than the criminals. It needs something extraordinary to invert a prejudice against the police into a presumption in their favour. But there they are, Botwright and Wootton, 'Two Men With A Thirst For Guinness', as the headline simperingly announces. They actually look like a couple of plods in plain clothes: in the picture, Botwright is wearing a City outfit and overcoat, but the Metropolitan Police psycho intensity of his gaze gives the game away. Wootton wears a bulky, lighter-coloured coat, leather gloves and a frown. He holds his arms slightly away from his body so that he can hit you more easily if you start to make trouble. These are not Peter Wimseys. These are two hard guys, much like any hard guys from the Force. What have they done to deserve this Dashiell Hammett, Central Casting frivolity?

Even the *Sunday Times* started to echo this tone. 'When the DTI inspectors launched their inquiry in December,' the *Sunday Times* wrote, 'Botwright had been warned that he would spearhead any criminal investigation. For five months he waited impatiently ... Once the information became available the Fraud Squad moved fast ... Officers chosen to work on the case come from a hard core of experienced Fraud Squad investigators ...' Instead of being accused of random assaults, racist abuse or knucklehead sexism — the staples of contemporary police news stories — the men from the Fraud Squad have become society's avengers. They're impatient. They move fast. They spearhead things. They're a crack team.

The Guinness affair was so big, so pruriently surprising, that substantial changes were taking place. Money was at the root of it all. So far as the DPP was concerned, there were too many associations between the Tory Government and the City. It was acceptable, both parties argued, to feel good about having money, about having a lot of money. But when the City's money turned out to be the motor of corruption, the Government had to make it clear that in its view there was good wealth and bad wealth; that you could be rich and still have moral priorities. It had to strike a balance.

On the other side, the common people of Britain can only sustain the view that the police are the heroic forces of justice, if the crime they're investigating is nothing less than appalling. Or at least, if the criminals are appalling. And the most appalling criminals are the rich ones. Bent rich people are the stuff of the most gloating, squalidly moralizing fiction. Even the police are preferable to a rich villain.

Back in the City, reactions were confused. The Guinness business wasn't like the Geoffrey Collier case. City people get all mixed up trying to explain it. Collier's greed was an impulse of selfishness, a collapse into illegality. It was obvious. Once the news of his crime came through, he tidied up his life with a written confession, parcelling up the moment of failure and presenting it like the return of a stolen painting. But Guinness was so sprawling and untidy that it gets hard to piece out the guilt among the people involved.

At the very start of the line of corruption, things are straightforward. Back in May 1985, an illiterate hate-note arrived in New York from Caracas. Among the rubbish of mistyped Hispanic-English ('. . . As is mantion on that letter if us customers . . . upon you investigating to the last consequecies . . .') was a tip-off to the SEC that someone in New York brokers Merrill Lynch had been insider dealing. A year later, Dennis Levine emerged as the man responsible. Ever inclined to regard information as negotiable rather than confidential, he grassed on his friend Boesky. By November 1986, Boesky was being charged with criminal offences. This is where Guinness comes in. Boesky releases the incriminating information in his conversations with the SEC. The SEC pass it on to the DTI – and here we are, back in 1987, at the start of the year.

The Fraud Squad mainly wanted to know about share price manipulation. Guinness had been trying to take over the Distillers company. Their bid was made in shares, rather than cash. If your shares are worth more than those of your rival bidder (in this case, the Argyll Group) then the shareholders of the target company will be more likely to take your shares. So how do you get your shares to increase in value? You persuade your friends to buy them up. Now, in the final weeks of the takeover bid, Guinness shares went up from 281p to 353p. This made them highly attractive to the Distillers shareholders, and so Guinness won the fight. If your friends and other interested parties buy your shares because they think of you as a good thing, or because you can persuade them that you are a good thing, then this is all right. Independent investors might support a bid by buying shares, precisely because they think the bid is good for all parties. These independent investors may form what is known as a 'Fan Club': acting from the best motives, they discreetly urge the bid towards their preferred conclusion.

If, however, the bidding company pays you to buy its shares, or offers to indemnify you against any losses, then you may find yourself in something called a 'Concert Party'. Concert Parties are against the law. Guinness, under Ernest Saunders, were principally in trouble because it was suspected that they might have organized their share price support in much this way. Boesky had supposedly been dealing on their behalf in New York.

Gerald Ronson, a man for whom the word tycoon might have been coined, bought £25m of Guinness shares during the fight. Ronson is a plutocrat. He owns Britain's second largest private company, the Heron Corporation. His personal fortune is guessed to be standing somewhere between £700m and £1bn. He would also have been holding a fee of £5.8m after Guinness's victory, if he hadn't given the money back. This huge sum was paid to him through a stockbroking intermediary called Tony 'The Animal' Parnes. The £5m was nominated as a 'success fee' if Guinness won the battle. In other words, Ronson was not just persuaded to buy Guinness shares; he was paid to do so. The extra £800,000 was to indemnify him against the fall in the value of his £25m shareholding when he sold it off, after the bid.

This contract for services rendered came to light at the beginning of 1987, when Ronson, aware of the heat from the burgeoning DTI inquiry, gave the money back to Guinness. The company was under new management by now. Ronson apologized to the new chairman, saying that he should 'never have succumbed to the request for support'. It's hard to fathom the motive behind this act. Like Collier's written confession, it was presumably an attempt to bundle up the past and expel it from his life. Unlike Collier's confession, it was also, presumably, meant to exonerate Ronson from blame. The apology was supposed to forestall punishment rather than invoke it. Collier could have told him – if this was his reasoning – that he was being either suicidally ingenuous or recklessly disingenuous.

There is another possibility, one which Webb likes to advance. This is the theory of minimum responsibility. 'Ronson's a busy man,' argues Webb, candidly. 'He picks up the phone one day, it's his stockbroker on the other end, and the stockbroker' (that is, Tony 'The Animal' Parnes) 'says, I think it would be a good idea if you put £25m into Guinness. They are going to win this battle. Incidentally, they'll pay you £5m as a bonus when they get through. Ronson, still busy, thinks to himself, if my stockbroker says it's all right, then I shall do it. And he puts in his £25m and gets back to running the Heron organization. That's the last he thinks of it.' The problem, according to Webb, with sifting through the causalities of Ronson's share purchase, is that people (the press, the rest of the world, people who don't understand) work backwards. Because the share deal has become so embarrassingly significant, we assume that it was significant at the time it happened. But no, says Webb. It was just another piece of short-term investment for Mr Ronson, the busy chairman of the Heron organization. And you can judge the worth of this interpretation by Ronson's reactions early in 1987. 'He gave the money back like that, with the note of apology, in broad daylight, everybody watching him, because he *wasn't guilty*. It wasn't something which he'd put a lot of himself into . . . he'd just said, yes, okay . . . then he wakes up one morning and there's this pile of money in the bank and he thinks, what am I doing with this?' The thing just sidles into Ronson's life, unseen by his nervously alert ethical self, and settles down . . .

This view gets nowhere with Lucky Paul. First, says Lucky Paul, Ronson couldn't have made a deal like that with Tony 'The Animal' Parnes without giving it some reflection. He was on top of the matter to the extent that he put in an invoice to Guinness after the bid: 'In due course our invoices were rendered . . . and these were paid,' said Ronson in early 1987. Secondly (and this is what rankles) Webb's analysis puts the burden of responsibility on Tony 'The Animal' Parnes. The busy tycoon is stitched up by the City professional. That is in bad taste, according to Lucky Paul.

The City's view of its part in the Guinness business shifts from beleaguered innocence to Mephistophelean guile. What *was* the City doing for Guinness? Didn't anyone suggest that as takeover battles went, this one was somewhat risky? Ask a pious City solicitor what the most prominent City advisers in the case *thought* they were doing, and he says, 'They probably acted in good faith . . . they gave the best advice they could . . . I'm sure that they wouldn't have consciously committed a wrong act . . .' Lucky Paul inclines to this childlike view of things, with modifications. His belief, or at least the belief he wills himself to hold, is that the ideas, the schemes, came from the business side. Successful businessmen, in Lucky Paul's world, are irresistible. This is how they get to be successful. They bend things shamelessly to their wills. The ethical fastidiousness that he, Lucky Paul, might feel about the things that businessmen do, is one of the reasons why he is a professional and they are entrepreneurs. Businessmen have no scruples about how they use other people (people like Seelig, Roux, Salz and so on). They compel the flinching City guys into doing things in a particular way. Get this job done, they insist, or you (and your grandee firm) will never work for me again. The City guys, crushed on one side by the compulsive businessmen and on the other by the huge, threatened prestige of their firms, give in.

Guinness, in particular, handed Lucky Paul and his confederate believers, a perfect hate object in the shape of Ernest Saunders. Everything about Ernest Saunders suggests to Lucky Paul that his priorities were deformed. Saunders had an exemplary beginning in life, one that Lucky Paul would have nodded at without a second thought. He was educated at St Paul's, and Emmanuel College, Cambridge. Ah, but before that — before the high-priced rectitude of St Paul's and Cambridge — he was *Schleyer*, not Saunders, the son of an immigrant Jewish gynaecologist from Vienna who came to England to escape persecution. Saunders was the new name, the immigrant's bid to lose himself and his family in the blessed liberalism of England. In other words, Saunders started off *not one of us*.

Later, he worked for J. Walter Thompson, the advertising agency. That was all right, except for the whiff of mania that starts to hang about him from this time. On his first date with the woman who was to become his wife, the story goes, he took her to inspect the sales positions given to J. Walter Thompson's clients' products, in certain London supermarkets. Instead of dancing to a jazz combo and drinking Chianti in the King's Road, they spent the evening checking toothpaste, tinned foods, soap powders.

Then follows an uninspiring catalogue of deeds done for his next employers, Nestlé of Geneva. This included channelling money through a Washington foundation to sway public opinion against the World Health Organization who were arguing that Nestlé's powdered baby milk was causing malnutrition in Third World countries.

And at last, he turns up at Guinness in 1981. He gets rid of 150 Guinness subsidiaries in two years, fires his old bosses, J. Walter Thompson, from the advertising account, and doubles the earnings per share in just over a year. Shareholders and members of the Guinness family thought he was terrific. Others thought he was a megalomaniac. He took into his club of advisers and schemers, a man from his old Nestlé days with the fabulous name of Arthur Fürer. At a dinner given by the Marketing Society, he stipulated that his table should be three feet higher off the ground than anyone else's. He gave a non-executive job to Sir Thomas Risk, Governor of the Bank of Scotland and celebrated for his correctness, to sweeten his board's public image. But he sacked Risk a few months later, for being tiresomely non-compliant. He was called 'Deadly Ernest'.

Lucky Paul naturally fears and dislikes ruthless businessmen. The nature of his work, however, compels him to subdue these bad feelings. So he suffers a protracted inner conflict which from time to time releases itself in a mixture of abusive snobbery ('... these company bosses ... they don't *know* anything ... and he's ... common ...') and misdirected anger ('... I'm going to get *him* ... he's getting a *panning* from me ...'). But when someone like Deadly Ernest snakes into Lucky Paul's world, then everything becomes easy. Saunders lets Paul off the hook. Everything is Saunders' fault because, as far as you can tell, just about everything *is* Saunders' fault. Lucky Paul doesn't go as far as a bug-eyed Nazi stockbroker who furtively insisted that 'The *whole thing* is a conspiracy: it's a conspiracy of the *North London Jewish Mafia* . . .'; but he does take the opportunity to heap as much of the blame as he possibly can on Saunders' shoulders.

Not everyone else sees it this way. Webb exculpates Gerald Ronson and the small matter of £5.8m by putting the blame at Tony 'The Animal' Parnes' door. And certainly, 'The Animal' left for America later in the year with Guinness's £3.5m fee in his briefcase and a 'For Sale' notice outside his smart Hampstead house (more than smart; supersmart, with an asking price of £4.5m) and an intention of starting a new life somewhere in Los Angeles. But then Webb is the kind of person to hold a grudge against a thrusting individualist, an anarch like 'The Animal', much as he heaps contumely on Seelig.

But the biggest problem that Webb identifies – and he shares this point of view with Nick the Lloyd's man and the Ace Merchant Banker – is the problem of tunnel vision. What does everyone else do? You do what they do. In a takeover battle the ethical grounds for action are about as vague as a pattern of clouds in the sky. Financial imperatives are only tied to ethical imperatives by the flimsiest bonds. The main thing is to win. That's what principally weeds out one course of action in favour of another. And if that's what people do, then that's what people do. The system defines itself by immediate, common practice, rather than by external principle. As you narrow the range of your specialization, so you narrow the ethical world you inhabit. Demon Keith has his rules; the LIFFE trader has his; Roger Seelig has his. There *is* no big hand coming out of the ceiling and touching your shoulder in admonition when you overstep the mark. There's only the person next to you.

Webb sits back and says, provocatively, 'The maxim is: if you're not lying, you're not trying.' When the team who organized the Guinness bid got together, they had no ethical conduit feeding in from the outside world. And if one member of the team steps firmly into a world of deception and concealment, his co-professionals, might not even notice a transgression which the outside world would seize on immediately. 'You're involved in a big takeover,' says the Ace Merchant Banker, 'sometimes it acquires a momentum of its own. You might be perfectly straight yourself, but, uh, once you start advising on these things, you just get – caught up . . .'

Is it tunnel vision? Is it a simple yielding to the driving force of competition? Is it corruption? Does it come from these opportunistic thugs called businessmen; or are most City professionals just waiting for the chance to cut corners, to cheat a little? Or is that only for the really successful ones?

Is it something in the air, an invisible shift in values which happens the moment you involve yourself in the City's world and which affects everyone working there? Is it this, more than anything else, that denotes the City as another country?

The City is bursting with decent folk who make it their responsibility to behave correctly in their professional lives; just as they broadly subscribe to the idea that theft is wrong, that violence is unjustifiable, that we should act humanely at all times. The City also contains people who can shelve their burden of propriety from time to time, in big things and in small things.

In fact, after a while, you start to feel bottomlessly naive, a knucklehead in the classroom of human understanding, when you ask the sixth or seventh City type whether the place is straight or crooked. Of course it's crooked! At least, *some* of it's crooked. What a question! How could it be anything else? Are we saints? So, Collier wasn't alone . . .? *Collier got caught.* That was what singled *him* out. And Guinness – and share price manipulation? Other people have done much the same. Who are these people? Well, one knows *of* these things, not necessarily dates and places. It just goes on.

Is the question even worth asking? You get two answers: either, City professionals (with one or two infamous exceptions) are straight, conscientious people; or, the City runs on expediency, not rectitude – deceit is the fuel of finance. Now, the first sounds specious (society just *isn't like that*), a lie. But if you believe the second answer, then the implications, are so huge, baleful, absurd, that you simply turn your back on the mountainous problem you have decided to face. Which is what the City does. The City, a great national profit-making institution, the centre of European financial expertise, the third great world financial market, the new age City, the meritocratic City, is *bent*? *Surely not*?

The nearest you might get to a formal justification for the way the City tends to act, is through some kind of comparison with, say, the legal profession. We know the queasiness with which lay people regard the lawyer's capacity for shedding his regular moral perspective in order to function as a lawyer; that willed mental distortion which enables a barrister wholeheartedly to defend a rapist, a killer, a mobster. We shudder at the solicitor's power to leave the ordinary world behind while he handles the paperwork for a chemicals company that wants to tip arsenic into the water table. The City's the same; we don't necessarily like doing some of the things we do, but that's how it is in finance. You can't expect all the scruples of everyday life to transfer themselves into this other world; you'd never get anything done. Professions tend to be morally complicated things. The City is like that. People do wrong things, but not *all* the time. It works as an institution, as Nick says about Lloyd's, riddled with shortcomings – but it *makes money*.

Yet it's hard to shake off one nagging thought. When doctors extend the boundaries of professional practice, they meet argued opposition, discussion in the learned journals, committee resolutions. When teachers sound out new ways of doing things, they arouse parental concern, education authority seminars, TV reports. If an architect comes up with a new building design, you have a public enquiry, a volley of letters to the newspapers. These days, when the City tries something a little different, it gets Botwright and Wootton from the Fraud Squad.

113

7

SUMMER: THE NERVOUS HEIGHTS

CONFIDENCE

The Prime Minister confirmed the date of the General Election. The opinion polls were rigidly optimistic. By the end of May, the Tories were anything between 10 per cent and 12 per cent ahead of Labour. The stock market stayed busy, heading for 2200 on the FOOTSIE.

There seemed to be so much loose money, that you could even make a profit out of the wreckage of Guinness. The Bank Leu, based in Zurich (Chairman, Arthur Fürer, Saunders' old colleague), was in possession of 40m Guinness shares. So they looked for someone to buy them. This was 40m shares, each worth between £3 and £4, perhaps £14m's worth. This was a real test of the City of the new age, the City with muscle.

The stockbrokers James Capel put in an offer of 350p a share and bought them all. Then they had to sell this mountain of equities. They put 100 dealers on the case, gave them a pep talk and let them loose on the institutional buyers. After ten minutes, they had sold the entire order at a price of 352p a share. They had coursed through the big purchasers and the block buyers and the elephantine pension funds and in the end persuaded 163 different institutions to take some Guinness shares. In ten minutes, they turned the deal round, and cleared a profit of £800,000. What was *that*? Superhuman placing power? Massively implausible luck? Tickling the desires of a monster of speculative greed?

Foreign investors alone were consuming more and more of the market. Back in 1982, they'd bought about £60m of British equities and £356m of UK gilts. By the end of 1986, these figures had exploded into £13.5bn's worth of gilts and £25bn in UK equities. This gave them 5 per cent of the total market. Americans and Japanese were getting keener to have a piece of any company that was in the top one hundred UK equities, and whose name began with 'British'. The more cosmopolitan Americans and Japanese were even prying into less familiar stocks. One or two City brokers took it upon themselves to jet salesmen out to Tokyo to explain the wordless pleasure of owning Black & Decker or Laura Ashley. The world wanted something from the UK equities market, and when James Capel opened up its warehouseful of Guinness shares they sold them in minutes. In fact, the placing was not just welcomed; it was over-subscribed *ten times.*

The odd suggestion of summer filtered through the cack of the City streets. The deranged little public gardens which still litter the City (round the backs of dead churches and semi-derelict umbrella factories) were bringing forth leaves and a few bleary flowers. Summertime drinking – standing on the pavement outside the Jamaica Inn, basking in the cloud of chop smoke which came out of Simpson's windows – became possible. The money was there. You could think about your summer break. Club Med in the West Indies? Thailand? We've got this house in Dorset . . .

BAD NERVES

But there were alarms. One of them was a joke – a faintly depressing joke, but still a joke – while another was a more serious tremor. The joke happened on Thursday, 4 June. A little group of City reprobates started a rumour that the forthcoming MARPLAN opinion poll, due for release at seven o'clock that evening, would show that the Tories' lead over Labour – a full 4 per cent according to the Gallop poll earlier that day – was down to 2 per cent. This jape turned into a convulsion of fear that seized so many traders that share prices fell by £6bn before the MARPLAN result duly appeared. It gave the Tories a 12 per cent lead. Had someone profited in the hours that the lie was abroad? High spirits, they said; scapegraces, exploiting the nerve of fear that ran through all the bumptiousness and beady profiteering. What the hell.

In the same week, Paul Volcker resigned his job as Chairman of the Federal Reserve Board. A crumpled-looking guy called Alan Greenspan took over. This was the tremor. The Federal Reserve Board is the United States' central bank, a Yankee Bank of England. Its chairman is a highly influential person. Now, although the Great Glutton had been rolling in a sty of consumption, expenditure, deficits, and fiscal incontinence for the past few years, the rest of the world was still ready to place its doubtful confidence in the system if the Chairman of the Federal Reserve Board gave an impression of weight and competence. Paul Volcker did that. He was incredibly tall — 6ft 7½in. without his shoes. He had a name for clearsightedness and intellectual rigour. This didn't seem to have helped the Great Glutton in any practical sense, but it was nice to know that this very tall man was in a position of responsibility. The Vice-President of Goldman Sachs, the Wall Street broking firm, described Volcker as 'a sort of financial demi-god'. When he resigned, it created a spasm of anxiety in the economic strategy departments of bankers and brokers throughout the City. Something was going to happen. You couldn't say quite *what* or *when*, but something was definitely going to happen. Volcker's quitting was an augury of the bad thing that would happen.

On 11 June, the Tories managed to win a 101-seat majority. The south of England voted Tory, with a few exceptions. Bernie Grant held Tottenham, in North London, for Labour. Paul Boateng did the same for Brent South and told a bemused world of the bond between his west London suburb and a South African township. Garlanded with a necklace of flowers, he announced, 'We can never be free in Brent until South Africa is free too. Brent South today, Soweto tomorrow . . .' Rosie Barnes, a market researcher with a fubsy smile, kept Greenwich for the haggard SDP/Liberal Alliance. Otherwise, everything went as expected.

Some of the City stayed awake for the whole of election night. Gilts and bonds dealers, whose products would be the most immediately prone to disintegration if the Tories lost, stayed at their desks, scratching and gibbering as the news items came in on their Reuters screens. The rest went home, apart from a core of happy yobs who remained in the bars. A nerveless reporter from *New Society* found herself in a scrum of traders fitfully hard at work around one o'clock on the Friday morning. They were struggling to keep dealing. One of them was so exhilarated with fear that he could only deal standing up, his trousers undone, his left hand anxiously rummaging around his testicles. Later on, she got into a taxi with a morbidly wretched banker called James. He explained that he was an emotional cripple and began to read her shreds of his own poetry, which he kept, revealingly, in his wallet.

Lucky Paul gawped at the television at home. It had been a busy day, and now there was this wrecky presenter in a pair of suede loafers shuffling backwards and forwards in front of a great wall of constituency names . . . like an immense SEAQ screen, showing Tory blue for a price rise and hysterical Labour red for a fall. Early in the morning, he was jolted out of his doze by a parade of darkies who gave him the clear impression that revolution was due in a couple of neighbouring London boroughs – Islington stayed faithfully Labour, and soon it would be time to go to work again.

The next day was full of relief. The City dreads any possibility of a Labour government, much as Labour dreads the City's reaction if it ever gets into power. In fact, it's not easy to know who fears the other more. The City, especially with a twitchy, Tory throng of Americans and Japanese at its centre, would sell the pound, mark billions off equity prices, and wilfully engineer a balance of payments crisis. A new Labour administration, on the other hand, could shackle investors' freedoms to invest, tinker with the conceptual differences between privatized, nationalized and quasi-nationalized industries, and double the income tax rates. The Americans and Japanese would leave for Amsterdam or Frankfurt or Paris. The London Docklands development scheme would fail and several importers of high-priced German and Italian cars would go out of business.

It would be a catastrophe. So, as for a nuclear war, or the explosion of an atomic reactor, the people in charge made contingency plans. Sometimes this involved keeping a 'stake-out' man in the office while everyone else went home. His job was to move all the firm's transferable assets to Singapore or Hong Kong the moment a Labour majority appeared. Other outfits, the market makers and dealers, simply cleared out their books and went into the night of

11 June with no shares at all. Smith New Court did as much, despite the opinion polls and the bull market. Their managing director of UK Equities said that he wanted to be a 'tiny, tiny bear', in case democracy brought home the wrong government. The possibility of being caught with a bookful of stock and a Labour administration was too painful for him to be anything else. He reckoned, for instance, that if the Tories got back in, British Telecom shares could go up by 15p. But if Labour won, BT could lose as much as 60 or 70p.

Warburg Securities, conversely, decided to brave it out. Their reasoning was that a Tory victory was likely; shares would go up (as the man from Smith New Court also presumed); anyone with stock to sell first thing on Friday morning would make money. A firm of brokers called Hoare Govett did the same. They were both rarities in the City. There was more fear than greed around, no matter what MARPLAN or MORI told them.

Then the huge Conservative majority duly arrived, and everyone knew there was a profit to be made. They had to manage the trick of time and circumstance, to magic money from chance. Warburgs started work at around 6.30 a.m., selling their (now guaranteed safe) stock. By 7.15 a.m., the FOOTSIE had gone up 47 points to a new peak of 2296.4. Once it had hit this target, it started to drop. The buyers were now selling, and prices were depressed, By lunchtime the FOOTSIE was no more than nine points up. Still, the chance had been there; somebody came out ahead. The only thing that didn't happen, was the 'Wall Of Money'. This was a speculators' fantasy that the Americans, and especially the Japanese, would be so gratified by a Tory win and the vision of four more years of profiteering that they would wade into the London Stock Market and buy tranches of shares in British companies. It was a fiction that somehow gained more and more currency as the election got nearer. Why should they invest so extravagantly in the hours immediately after a Conservative return? Well, they just would.

They didn't. Like the phoney opinion poll rumour which took £6bn off the market in half a day, like the inexplicable small crash in April, like the bull market itself, the 'Wall Of Money' was an idea that got around, rather than a reason to anticipate something. The Japanese didn't stop buying things, but they didn't go on an orgy of share buying, either. 'I suppose,' a rueful optimist confessed on the Friday, 'it was unrealistic to suppose they would do anything so unsubtle.'

But the Tories held on. Another hectic moment passed. The confidence trick was still working.

KEEPING IT GOING

What was happening, now? You have to watch out for the distortions of hindsight. Were things getting more nervous, more pushy? Did anyone suspect anything? An analyst might sift through the compost of charts, predictions, commentaries, statistics and omens of the period and acknowledge that something *was* souring. But at the time, you couldn't stop. Every day, the analysts disgorged another cargo of essays and reports. Some were bullish, some were mealy mouthed. The economists might have told you that share prices were outrageously overvalued, the US economy was shot, the prospects for world trade looked poor, but then this was like so much static in your mind, the babble of expertise. You had to go on. There was more money waiting to be made. The sun shone from time to time, the weather was warmer than in winter, things were, probably, on balance, better than they used to be.

There were also various straightforward things you could do to keep the Stock Market busy (and business, as long as it didn't consist of repeated sells and no buys, was what you wanted). Lucky Paul, for instance, takes a pride in his ability to move share prices about. 'I get a thrill — I get a real pleasure from seeing a share price move as a result of a recommendation that I've made,' he says. 'I look at the Stock Exchange share prices in the morning, and I know that half of them are wrong. The best thing about this job, is being able to make a visible difference to the way the market behaves. That's really satisfying.'

Now, Webb covertly despises this philosophy. It's immature, he maintains — not because he has an ethical objection to people who try to manipulate market forces for their own private satisfaction, but because he hates that kind of egotism. He looks about and shuffles his impure hair with his fingers. 'Some people get a kick out of it. I think that anybody who does so should *break the habit*.' But then, Webb has a habit of his own, according to Lucky Paul, which is even less endearing. This is called churning. Webb gets seriously annoyed if you ask him about churning. It sounds emetic, but all it means is that the broker takes a private client's portfolio and fiddles aimlessly with it to generate a commission for himself and, coincidentally, more business all round. Depending on the kind of discretionary powers the client invests in his broker, a Webb can churn a portfolio without even getting his client's approval. He can even take two similar portfolios and merely swap the contents over. No application of the intelligence, no effort, just a double commission at the end. That's the beauty of churning.

Webb doesn't do it! It's a repellent practice. It brings the profession into disrepute! Well, if Webb doesn't do it, there are others who do, Lucky Paul claims. Lucky Paul and Webb are working for the same firm, doing business in the same part of the City, but Webb's rooted dislike of Paul's vanity and Lucky Paul's high-minded scorn for what he is certain Webb gets up to, drive a wedge between them.

Nor can they agree on front-running. This is yet another way to stay in profit. Front-running is one of those activities that looks as if it ought to make some kind of clear ethical sense, but which keeps squirming out of focus. Front-running is another simple practice. You are a stockbroking firm. You have an analyst who does his job diligently and well, and he decides that Amalgamated Consolidated Plc are undervalued by the market and would make a good addition to anyone's portfolio of investments. So the analyst gives Amalgamated Consolidated a fine write-up: 'The company is in an excellent position ... attractive development programme ... the necessary finance is in place ... sustained rapid growth ... Buy without hesitation...' The report is ready to be circularized to the big investors; the big investors, the life assurance companies, the fund managers ring up and demand a share of Amalgamated Consolidated Plc. What happens if you don't have any shares on your books? How do the big investors get hold of the shares? Do they go somewhere else? Do you have to shop around trying to meet customer demand, and finding that as you do so, the price creeps up and up?

No. You go in for front-running. You buy in a consignment of Amalgamated Consolidated shares before the report ever goes out. Then you tell your customers the news about the company. They put in their orders with you, which you obediently satisfy. You, of course, have bought the shares cheap and now sell them at a profit. Of course you do, complains Webb. That's what a broker's in business to do. It's naive to think that anything else would be the case. But Lucky Paul's argument intervenes. What you have just done is manipulate the market to create a profit for yourself. You haven't anticipated a movement in the share price; you've created it and capitalized on it. Webb sees this (at a distance; he doesn't actually say this to Paul's face) as the gesturing of a business innocent. What is the good of telling somebody that something is wonderful if you can't let them buy it? And Lucky Paul retorts that it's not like advertising; it's not as if there are competitive products involved. There is only one company, one share, one product. And you have temporarily made yourself the most accessible supplier.

Front-running is not as seedy, however, as using the press to do a little share ramping for you. Now this is where Webb and Lucky Paul can agree. 'There's nothing easier than to ramp a share price,' Webb explains, 'by going into a pub where the press hang about, and muttering Amalgamated Consolidated ... blah blah ... Yield ... blah blah ... Surprise in store ... and they tear off and write it down, and the next day out it comes in the papers. When a City PR firm does this with the Sunday papers, it's known as the *Friday Drop*. That's what Webb maintains, and Lucky Paul sides with him. It's a cheap and disreputable practice. But what about Lucky Paul's faith in the popular press? Remember the hotline it gave the small investor? What does this kind of ramping mean for him? Has Lucky

Paul dug himself another pit of inconsistency? 'Well, it *can* be a good thing. You *can* get some good tips from the newspapers. You don't *have* to, though.' And so from time to time, a broker may put in a less than accurate story, thanks to the drugged credulity of a journalist he recognizes, and will perhaps shift a line of B-grade stock into the hands of investors who don't know any better? Absolutely not! You're not that cynical about your work. No one is. Except, of course, for Webb, who nods wearily and lights a cigarette. 'These things happen. You do what you can to keep the turnover up.'

(Other people have other ways of keeping their turnover up. At around this time, a firm called LHW Futures were suspended from the London Commodity Exchange and refused membership of the Association of Futures Brokers and Dealers. LIFFE had also refused them membership in 1986. They had something of a name for hard selling. Back in 1984, an investor who claimed to be 'fairly sophisticated financially' ended up losing £19,247 in six weeks, thanks to LHW's commodity broking department. They telephoned him so persistently and so enthusiastically that he bent under the pressure, invested according to their plans and lost more or less everything. A couple of years later, much the same happened to a man in Wolverhampton, who lost £15,000 speculating in futures through LHW. A couple in Wales lost £27,000. What made it worse, was that LHW took a total of £32,000 in commission on these last two deals, thanks to an arrangement which gave them a non-returnable 25 per cent of all the money put up by their investors. Their remorseless telephone sales technique was given as the reason why the speculators had paid the money in the first place. Dutifully, LHW then announced that they would review their methods of selling and charging commission, in the future. But while it lasted, it really kept things going.)

You'd like to imagine the City at this time as something from *Under The Volcano* or *Rain*: 'A hothouse, seething, humid, sultry, breathless, and you had a strange feeling that everything was growing with a savage violence ...' Actually, the weather had been appalling. The sun didn't shine, it was cold, and there was rain; not Somerset Maugham's tropical variety but a miserable, futile kind that took the creases out of your trousers and made your hair smell like a horse blanket. There wasn't that much loafing about outside the Jamaica Inn with a lager in your hand, simply because it was too cold and wet. But the FOOTSIE was still rising: by early July, after a raid on the market by some big buyers, the Index stood at 2328.1. There is a tired Stock Market adage about selling in May and buying back on St Leger Day, which accounts for the traditional slump in prices around midsummer. This didn't seem to be happening. The FOOTSIE at least was feverish.

But even as the FOOTSIE rose, the UK trade figures for May came out, and they were abysmal. There was a deficit of £1.16bn, double that for April. Moreover, the market had risen 48 per cent in value since 2 January, and the chartists − (those analysts who use mathematics and graphs, rather than educated guesses, to make their predictions) said that a correction, in other words a fall − was due. There was also a lot of material for the market to absorb: more than £12.4bn had been released on to the Stock Market since the turn of the year, all in rights issues, flotations and privatizations. The market needed a deluge of money to accommodate all this new paper. Perhaps the rush for Bank Leu's Guinness shares was an aberration. Eventually, soon even, the market would just glut itself and stop buying.

The American Economy was in no better condition than before. Not only that, but some commentators were already discussing what kind of emergency action the more productive economies (Germany and Japan, basically) would have to take to bail out the Great Glutton when matters went seriously wrong. They tended to conclude that Germany's neurotic anality and Japan's hyper-complicated financial dynamics weren't going to be enough to save America.

But what could you do? No one was in any position to bail out of the Stock Market simply because bad times might be coming. Nor did enough people feel certain that things would change *that soon*. You deal in weeks, a month, no more than that. The Stock Market is kept alive by a continuous battle between will and knowledge. Its adepts have learnt how to willingly suspend their disbelief.

THE PROSPERO OF MONEY, AGAIN

One man, at least, had decided to quit. Remember Sir James Goldsmith? Remember Goodyear, back in November, and the $93m clear profit from a deal that never even happened? Remember the Prospero of money, the man who could magic it out of the air? At the end of July, he started to clear out.

He began with his New York offices. He'd come to America late in his career, and he was obviously happy to let it be the last in, first out. There were reports that he was 'running down' the US operation. Chattering speculators wondered if he was going to 'retire from active business life'. There was a certain amount of platitudinizing about Sir James Goldsmith's 'mercurial temperament' and his Quixotic approach to life. A couple of weeks later, he sold 95 per cent of his holdings in Générale Occidentale, his most important and prestigious company, the one which everybody associated with Sir James Goldsmith. It took a lot to buy him out. A group of purchasers led by the Compagnie Générale d'Electricité had to find £151m to complete the deal. He was even supposed to be releasing his 40 per cent share in a London club run by John Aspinall. He was whittling himself down to nothing but an island of pure money.

Why? 'Jimmy gets bored.' 'Sir James likes the challenge of starting new ventures, not the tedium of overseeing them year after year.' 'Sir Jimmy's planning something new and very exciting for which he needs a mountain of cash.' 'He's whimsical, capricious, unconventional.' 'He thinks the market's going to crash, and he wants to get his money out *now* . . .' This was the man who started the *Annus Mirabilis* with $93m of magic. This was the man who could make things happen just by letting you know he was *thinking* of making things happen. Did he know something? Clearly, the Compagnie Générale d'Electricité were happy enough to sponsor his departure. No one else was selling up. Robert Maxwell, Rupert Murdoch, Sir Phil Harris weren't selling off their businesses. They couldn't, anyway; the markets would have disintegrated under the pressure. Sir James Goldsmith seized the moment to quit, and if anyone else had been thinking about it, they were simply too late.

On 15 July, the FOOTSIE reached 2443.4. That is a substantial figure, especially when you recall that at the start of January it had been around 1680 and *that* had seemed substantial at the time. But in the second week of August, it broke down.

The Chancellor of the Exchequer had put interest base rates up from 9 per cent to 10 per cent, on Thursday 6 August. This scared the City. The FOOTSIE at once dropped 56 points on the Thursday and another 65 points by Friday lunchtime. After picking up a few points on Friday afternoon, it was still left with its biggest-ever weekly fall: down 134 points, at 2226.2. The newspapers dipped blindly into the well of cliché; 'Black Thursday' and 'Black Friday' were coined. Was this the bad thing, the fruit of Volcker's departure from the Federal Reserve Board, the Great Glutton's failing economy, the UK trade figures for May, was this the pit into which everyone would fall?

A week later, the index had picked up 69 points, and was resting comfortably enough at 2295.4. Black Thursday? Black Friday? It turned out that there had been no need to get *too* excited. The latest UK trade and inflation figures were better than most people had anticipated. The bad thing that Lawson's base rate rise had notionally cloaked wasn't there. It was an attack of nerves.

But there was a bad thing: the City itself. The London Stock Market, now looking more and more terminally fat, unhealthy and prone to hysteria, had seen the rise in base rates and abreacted. This is not, supposedly, what the London Stock Market is there for. The Wall Street and Tokyo markets had both gone on their ways quite unconcerned about London; the Dow Jones was up 27.59 on the week, the Nikkel Dow up 312.84. This was a purely domestic crisis.

Whom do you blame? One theory blames the theorists – the economists, the analysts, the Lucky Pauls, the nifty ruminants and pencil-chewers from Britain's universities; these people had failed to make the right prognosis. Shearson Lehman's analysts, for example, were predicting a £750m balance of trade deficit; Phillips & Drew's team, £700m. The actual figure turned out to be £168m.

No one is perfect, but then you have to balance that truism

against the analysts' status within the firms they work for. These thinkers powerfully represent the rationality of the new age. You listen to what the guys say. You don't wangle your way out of trouble by the old intuitive feelings you get in your stomach; you pay attention to the analysts. And if they say that everything is due to get worse, you act on it and *sell*. Now, some of their guesses are accurate guesses; some aren't. But what the theorists are not good at is anticipating the consequences of their intellection in the market overall. They don't so much mismanage their bad news; as fail to manage it at all.

Another theory also gained popularity. It blamed the market makers, the dealers themselves. And it certainly looked as if the dealers had been lax. One of the things they were supposed to have done was not answer the phone when trading became unpleasant. Before the Big Bang, when jobbers worked on the floor of the Stock Exchange and met face to face with the brokers they had to deal. If you claimed to be buying and selling shares in a company, you had your prices marked up next to you. You could not hide when a broker came up to you and demanded to sell thousands of unsellable shares; you had to make a trade. But now your market maker, your jobber, sits by a telephone to do his business. And if he suspects, as will happen in a market slump, that someone is trying to get hold of him to sell a parcel of equities that no one could possibly want, then he may just refuse to answer his phone.

This was one story. Once again, no one can agree on how true it is. Brokers and investors are still happy to complain about the slovenliness of the dealers. They know that there were some dealers who weren't answering; they're convinced that some market makers had taken fright, and had decided to sit on their hands until things quietened down. (Of course it happens – everyone knows someone to whom it happened, even someone who was guilty. If you don't believe it, you are blind to human nature.) The market makers, on the other hand, will deny the crime until death; it's just possible that some miscreant somewhere was inattentive, and failed to answer his phone when he should have; but ninety-nine per cent, (believe me) of all the dealers worked hard and conscientiously to mop up stock and keep the market liquid. Anyway, how would you react if the market was falling 15 points every hour and you had a bundle of fairly speculative stock on your books? You'd cover yourself. You wouldn't take chances. Would you have the balls to cope?

Besides, a Stock Exchange spokesman announced frostily on the day after Black Friday, 'We only received one complaint on this count on Friday. If stockbrokers find they cannot deal with a market maker, they should report the matter to our Supervisory Committee.' The only difficulty with this as a general retort, according to a stockbroker, is that if you complain to the Supervisory Committee about one of the market makers, then when business returns to normal, that market maker may refuse to deal at all sensibly when he has some stock that you want to buy off him. So you are inclined not to make a formal complaint, and the practice goes on. In this case, the practice may have added a billion or two to the £7bn the market lost in value on Friday morning.

Other things seemed to be faulty too. One of the reasons why the market had gone up so fast, was also one reason why it went down fast. This was the strange invisible force of inter-dealer trading. Before Big Bang, the jobber stood at his pitch on the floor of the exchange, and was his own man. He had his book of stocks and shares and he sold them and bought them as the stockbrokers moved around the floor. But now, thanks to SEAQ and the intervention of technology that Demon Keith and his race have provided, there are thirty or more market makers instead of the thirteen original jobbers on the Stock Exchange floor, and they can all deal with each other on their screens. No one needs to wait for a broker to come up with a 'buy' or 'sell' to start moving their stock around. 'You got some Plessey at 150? *Mine.*' 'You want some Greene King at 490? *Mine.*' 'Ladbrokes, anybody? *Mine.*' And so on. No brokers, no investors, no outside necessities to drive the thing on; just market makers making markets to balance their books, make a little turn on the deal, take a profit on a quiet speculation. That sends the market further and further up, when the mood is for buying; and it pushes it back down when everyone wants to sell.

One dealer, from a firm called Savory Milln, described what happened when he sold 25,000 building shares in the middle of the slump. No brokers or outside investors wanted them at the time, and the dealer to whom he'd sold them, didn't really want them either, and wasn't prepared to wait for a purchaser to come in from the outside world. So he sold them to another dealer over SEAQ, who sold them again to another dealer on SEAQ, who sold them again to another dealer ... The man from Savory Milln who had started this panicky traffic watched the price quotes on his SEAQ extension, and each time, the price moved down as one dealer after another took it on and then decided he didn't want it after all. After about an hour of this, the shares had fallen by 7p. This in turn meant that the company had lost one twentieth of its value, in an hour of fidgety punting, purely by the dealers among themselves. Now you couldn't have done that on the old floor of the Stock Exchange.

It was emerging that not enough people knew how to manage the market. Along with all the other inner calculations and blind guesses that a dealer has to cope with, he owes a broader duty to the market. This is a novel idea to many young dealers. A modern dealer can have a strictly limited view of his obligations. He has, he thinks, to keep his own book straight; he has a loyalty of some kind to his employers (whoever *they* are — some fuzzy cabal of Swiss penny pinchers, a backroom full of Chinese); he doesn't want to mess things up for his immediate colleagues. But the market? Who is the market? If prices go up, then that's what prices do. If they go down, someone, somewhere loses (I hope it's not *me*; I hope the Swiss anal neurotics and the bestial Chinks keep paying *me*). That's all the market is.

Old players, of course, have a different understanding of the operations of the market. It has, or had, two personalities. It reflected the ambitions or dreads of the outside investors. It moved the way others wanted it to move. But in the old days, when jobbers were their own men and had hexagonal beige pitches on the floor of the Exchange, the market also controlled the limits of fear or hope. That, anyway, is the principle. Jobbers acted in such a way that frightened investors had time to reconsider before they tried to sell everything and flee. They also had none of this inter-dealer business. Prices were regulated both by the jobber's mood, and the purchaser's desires, rather than by the jobber's terror or greed alone. This sort of approach helped to regulate the market. It put fetters on the worst kinds of emotions. The well-run market gave some kind of stability back to the investor.

Kleinwort Grieveson actually let it be known that they were putting this abstraction into practice, when they hired some ex-commodity traders to give sinew to their equities dealers. These old men had seen the worst horrors of the commodity markets, the ones where fortunes shrivel up like burning tissue when things go wrong. They knew how to cope with fear, and they understood the dynamic relationship between individual dealer panic and overall market collapse.

There is a generation gap between those who were around for the dreadful Bear Market of the 1970s and those who came into the City ten years later and know only the Bull Market and the crazily existential impulses of screen dealing. And there is a new spirit on the modern dealing floor, with its fidgeting yobs, its layabouts, its sweltering fatties with their arms crooked round to the backs of their necks and a half-eaten burger in a polystyrene clam open in front of them . . . For years, these people have been betting on the Bull Market with a float provided by their munificent sponsors, and no thought for the future. Some of them are Lucky Pauls, swept into the place by the greedy suction of the early 1980s. Some of them are one-time office gofers from bad schools who showed the latent fire of dealing and were trained up on a desk. Some are dreary suburbanites with telescopic umbrellas. Some are even women.

Whoever they are, they don't *know* that much. In the frenzy of overstaffing for the new age, just about anybody could get a job somewhere, and after a few weeks, might be left to run a place at the battery pen. After a few months, they might have several million pounds to job in and out of stocks and gilts. After a year, they even might be good at the task of riding the Bull. They might reckon themselves well worth the sixty grand plus car plus cheap mortgage that their bosses pay them. They might think they're, frankly, wonderful. But the *market?* What's that? You look after number *one*, boy.

By the time the slump had finished its work, the market was down by £25bn. Sir Nicholas Goodison called for an Inquiry into the matter of the unanswered telephones. It looked to some of the senior executives in the dealing houses and the high-rise multinationals as if the younger players needed more discipline. Is this what the market does when the nerves get too bad? Is this what happens when the confidence trick fails for a moment? Do all these disorders suddenly emerge from the exotic machines and the brilliant young people who work them? Did we plan for this? And what do we do if our nerve fails again?

THE CITY KEEPS CALM

What was left of summer drizzled on. The City went away for its rest cures in the South of France, the West Indies, Kenya, California and Turkey. We can allow Lucky Paul two weeks in a rented cottage in the Auvergne, while Webb goes to Sardinia and cuts his foot on a sharp stone. The Ace Merchant Banker and his girlfriend fly out to the States to stay with her brother.

It came back, to busy itself with the BP flotation (now going for some £7.5bn of investor's money and subtitled 'Be Part Of It'). It fooled around with various efforts to buy up Sir Terence Conran's group, Storehouse. One of these was coordinated by a private merchant banker called Peter Earl and an industrial concern with a name like a cough mixture, Benlox. This enterprise, worth £45m was planning to swallow up and then dismantle a concern valued at around £2bn. It kept many people happy, in the damp summer evenings, to wonder how Benlox would manage it, and how Sir Terence Conran would fight Benlox off. What a trick! That really *is* a confidence trick!

The merchant bank Hill Samuel was eaten by the Trustee Savings Bank. Tony 'The Animal' Parnes was by now imprisoned in Terminal Island Detention Centre, Los Angeles, while Scotland Yard tried to extradite him to present him with various charges of false accounting. Morgan Grenfell spent some time wondering if they were about to be taken over. The dollar stumbled lower and lower against the rest of the world's currencies. The FOOTSIE went up, to over 2360.

8

OCTOBER 1987: THE CRASH

HURRICANE

Looking back on it, the symbolism of the thing is almost vulgar: on Friday 16 October, the great storm struck. Three days later, the *Annus Mirabilis* ended in confusion. It was like something out of the opera house.

The night of 15 October was a dreadful night. A blast of air came up from the English Channel at around 100 mph, and scrambled in across south-east England. Londoners had gone to bed comforted, as ever, by Michael Fish, the most consoling of all TV weathermen, only to shake themselves out of sleep at 2.30 a.m. when the roof started to come away in chunks, and the municipal trees in the street outside began to crack. Anyone listening to the midnight forecast on Radio 4 would have heard that a serious gale was on the way, but a serious gale in southern England is no more than a stiff breeze to anyone from the land of the Kansas Twister or the China Sea Typhoons.

In London, the wind reached 94 mph. the highest authenticated speed since records began. This technically puts it in the 'Hurricane' class of the Beaufort Scale, at Beaufort force 12. 'Winds of this force,' the Beaufort table reminds us, are 'only encountered in tropical revolving storms . . .' In Hastings, a fisherman was killed by a flying beach hut. At Marston, in Kent, the wind averaged 69 mph for over ten minutes; to stand still in such a storm was like standing up through the sunshine roof of your car while you drove at the maximum legal speed down a motorway — if you stayed indoors, it was like driving your *house* at the maximum legal speed down a motorway.

By morning, the storm had killed nineteen people, brought down 15m trees and done £500m of damage.

The City was flattened too. Although the Stock Exchange stayed nominally open, SEAQ was out because of the power failures. Not only that, but the phones came and went as British Telecom's engineers fussed over cables and exchanges. Not many people got to work anyway. Either the trains were cancelled (no power; dozens of trees sprawled across the tracks) or their cars were penned in by wreckage. Millions of Londoners looked out in the dreary seven o'clock twilight at an unlit, immobile city they'd never seen before. Even the radio stations were on emergency power. LBC croaked away from a mobile broadcasting van, offering a dazed commentary of throat-clearings, baffled silences and sudden visions of the world outside. In the end, the City decided that Friday the 16th was not working. The FOOTSIE was suspended, and everyone went home.

The next day, *The Times* quoted a Meteorological Office spokesman, who said, wretchedly, 'We failed to realize the rapid way in which the depression was deepening . . .' The irony is deafening: 'we failed to realize . . .' The headlines on page one shouted 'Wasted Warnings Of The Storm'. A little lower down, in rather smaller letters, it said, 'Share Trading Suspended In The City'. And on one side, in a little column to the left, it announced in very small letters, 'Wall Street Suffers Worst Fall'.

The Dow Jones index had actually been stumbling quite badly during the whole of that week. On Wednesday, it lost 95.46 points, setting a new record at the time. On Thursday, it fell 57.61. Then it crashed by over a hundred on Friday. The total loss for the week, was 235.48 points, nearly 10 per cent of the total market value. A lot of colourful anecdotal chatter accompanied this news. Somebody at Shearson Lehman Brothers was supposed to have stuck a metal notice over one of the trading desks; it read 'To The Lifeboats' and bore an arrow pointing to the exit. Dealers and analysts were ripe with quotes: 'My guts are numb'. 'It's unreal, it's just unreal.' 'We have young traders here with their eyes popping out of their heads.' 'We are seeing clients come in with thousands of shares for sale, and they are not even taking a deep breath.' 'The Bull is dead.' 'I've been in the business thirty-three years, and it's one of the worst corrections I have ever seen.' There was a mood of transparent horror and surprise drifting like bad weather over the Atlantic.

What set it off? The first explanations were all to do with America's raging fiscal incontinence. On Wednesday, the US trade figures, came out. Not only were they worse than anyone had expected, they were worse than expected for the third month running. July's trade deficit had been $16.5bn. For August, the analysts and economists had pitched their estimates somewhere between $13bn and $15bn. The August figures which appeared on Wednesday admitted to a $15.7bn deficit. Manufactured exports were also down, by 3.7 per cent even though the falling value of the dollar (and the consequent cheapness of the American goods) should have increased the total. They were terrible figures. But they did not account for the crash.

THE CRASH

The confidence trick stopped working on what the press unambitiously named Black Monday. The Great Crash of 1929 started on Wall Street on 24 October; Black Thursday. What is it about October? you wondered. Something to do with the deadening approach of winter?

There were differences. One of the most visible distinctions between the crash of 1929 and the one of 1987 was the speed at which events took place. Although the first great wave of panic appeared on Black Thursday in the 1929 version, it only lasted until lunchtime. After that, a rescue committee, including the Chairman of the Chase National Bank and the Senior Partner of J. P. Morgan and Company, combined their funds and stopped the fall. The J. P. Morgan Senior Partner announced that things were 'susceptible to betterment'. Morgan's floor trader Richard Whitney went out after the committee had met, and marched from pitch to pitch, buying shares in one company after another until enough goodwill had returned to the floor of the exchange and life could go on. By the end of the day, the *New York Times* index of industrial stocks was down, but only by 12 points. It took a while for the thing to develop.

In London, on Monday, 19 October, it only took a few hours for the FOOTSIE to lose 249.6 points: the equivalent of £50bn in value. Back in 1929, there had been a continual problem with the ticker-tape machine. It was too slow to mark the price changes as they happened, so that investors who consulted it found themselves staring at prices that were already an hour or more out of date. This, it is said, contributed uniquely to the general sense of fear and hopelessness. But in Big Bang London, gimmicked up with its £46bn of hardware, this dislocating collapse of certainty couldn't have happened.

But it did. It still takes seconds for a trade to be marked up on the screen, or for a price to be quoted. And you can still think faster than TOPIC or SEAQ. So, once prices started to fall badly, even the SEAQ quotations were notional rather than actual. If you saw someone quoting Amalgamated Consolidated at 170, and tried to sell your holding of 20,000 shares, the chances were that in the time it took to get through, the price was already off to 165 or 162 or worse. How much was anything worth? As in 1929, you could only guess.

Everyone's screens turned red. All you could do was sit there and contemplate the end of the Bull, the expectancies of January and May, the 40 per cent of extra fat your shares had put on since the start of the year, the bonuses, the greed. The screens were red. On Friday the 16th, the FOOTSIE stood at 2301.9. By the end of Monday the 19th, it was down to 2052.3. On Wall Street, things were even worse: the Dow Jones Index lost 22 per cent of its value, falling 508.32, to 1738.4. The Chairman of the New York Stock Exchange ransacked his imagination for a suitable trope and came up with 'financial meltdown'. There was nothing but red, wherever you looked. What's more, no one had a strategy, because no one genuinely understood why the crash was happening. Abysmal trade figures. Yes. US bank lending rates going up. West Germans putting up their interest rates, choking off the world economy that little bit more to the Americans. Maybe. The prospect of fuddled, deaf, inconsequential President Ronald Reagan gaffing his way through another year or so of fiscal daydreams and Captain America defence spending was appalling. But you knew all this anyway. This, or something like it, had been going on for months. You could have guessed at it in August, and had the crash then. None of these was an answer; just another way into the same question.

The worst thing about the opening stages of the Great Crash of 1987 was that it was happening simply because it was happening; you were frightened because everyone was frightened. You took your lead, not from some greater external knowledge but, just as in the world of ethics, from the person on the other end of the line, or from the colleague next to you. You were locked into a psychological loop.

If Black Monday was bad, Tuesday was slightly worse. The FOOTSIE managed to drop a new record of 250.2 points in one day. This meant a loss of £43.7bn in share values, to add to the £50bn lost the day before. At the same time, a mythology was starting to grow out of the mess. Old hands who'd been in the City for more than twelve years found knots of university kids and bumptious tyros gathering around them. 'You were there in 1974,' they'd say. 'What was it like? Was it as bad as this?' And the old hand (all of thirty-five, maybe, but feeling like Lord Shinwell) would have to decide what kind of truth to tell them.

In one sense, the crash of the 1970s was far worse, because it took so long. The months of dwindling prices, all the way down to 146 on the old FT 30 Index, were a chronically painful annihilation. This thing, on the other hand, this epilepsy, was terrible in its own way. No one had ever seen it happen before, and that alone made it shocking. And if you let yourself contemplate the idea that it might fall not just fast but far, it was too vertiginous. So the old hands would tell the kids that it was unlike the crash of 1974, but nonetheless horrifying. This gave them something to chew over, as they marked down every price they could think of before some fund manager rang up to scuttle his holdings in ICI or British Telecom. They could look on this crash as their own, and start working up the tales they would tell their ingenuous contemporaries and their children.

Hong Kong had it worse, though. There the Stock Exchange collapsed completely. On Friday the 16th, the Hang Seng Index stood at 3738.2. By the end of Monday the 19th, it was down to 3362.39. Now, the players in Hong Kong are thought of as a rabble of crazy Chinese guys who are prone to gamble on anything that moves. They are *excitable*; even more excitable than the barking New Yorkers or the London foreign exchange dealers. So when the Hang Seng fell 420 points, it made a kind of sense. Unfortunately, there was not only a lot of money riding on the Hang Seng Index of share prices, but also on the Hang Seng Index futures market. There were over 84,000 Hang Seng Index contracts open; this was, in fact, the second biggest futures contract in the world. Speculators had been putting their money on the figure going up, or at least, not going down. And now there were fortunes waiting on the next move of the Hang Seng Index, and if it continued to drop, a lot of futures gamblers were going to be wiped out. The Hong Kong Stock Exchange panicked and closed down while they tried to work out what would happen if all these investors couldn't pay their bills. There was a rumour that more than £1bn of bad debts were behind the futures market. While New York, London and Tokyo went on posting their close of trading daily figures, Hong Kong put up 'Suspended' and left it at that.

If you were holding shares in Jaguar, one of the great original privatization successes, they would have looked like this: their high point in 1987 was at 632p. By 16 October, they'd fallen somewhat to just over 580p. Come Black Monday, and the price was down to 507p. On Tuesday, the day of the 250 point crash, the price fell by nearly a pound. Wednesday picked Jaguar up to 448p, and then Thursday knocked them out again, pushing them back down to 409p. The rest of the market, as filtered through the FOOTSIE, was having much the same kind of life. On Wednesday the market went *up* by 142 points. Wall Street did much the same, rising by 102. Then, Thursday came along, and the FOOTSIE buckled by over 190 points by the mid-afternoon, before it hauled itself back up to a negligible 110 point loss on the day. Christ, the traders and brokers thought, give us the weekend. Just let us go home. Friday gave in at 1,795.2 — a mere 38 point drop.

And that was that for the week of Black Monday. The price of equities, as expressed through the FOOTSIE, had gone from 2301 to 1795. Your Jaguar shares (if you still had any) were now worth less than £4.00. You could see them, your share certificates, sitting in a drawer in your desk, or in a stiff card folder, and the little beggars had shrivelled by £1.80 in the space of a week. You had £15,000 of Jaguar shares perhaps? You now had £10,300 invested in Jaguar, and the price, although interrupted by the hollow-eyed weekend, was still going down. The whole market had lost 22 per cent of its worth. And the weekend would come to an end, and the markets would open up on Monday (led, perhaps, by a scorched Hong Kong Stock Market) and then prices would just continue going down.

The Hong Kong Stock Market did open up again, on Monday 26 October. Before the market had been suspended the Index stood at 3362.39. By the close on Monday, it was down to 2241.69. This was a fall of 1120 points. One third of the market's value vanished in eight hours. The City contemplated Hong Kong's disintegration. The weekend had gone by, no one was much wiser or happier, and the reasons for savaging share prices, whatever they were, seemed as pressing as they had done before. So the FOOTSIE crashed once more, to show a loss of more than 150 points by lunch time, before regaining a few pounds in value, and closing down 111.1 at 1684.1. The New York Exchange opened up in a condition of bleak neurosis. The atmosphere was so dreary that the Dow Jones Index was able to record its second largest one-day fall of 156.83 points.

These eddies and currents of share price depreciation seemed unstoppable. Just when you thought everything was settling down it started up again. The Dow Jones' imperceptible drop of 0.33 points on Friday the 23rd had been explained away as the product of 'exhaustion', as if the index really were a thinking organism, a thing with volition, with preferences of its own. This was a way of dealing with the problem of the market's wayward collective psychology, by projecting it onto the index itself. That's how it is with indexes; they're like shaky prize fighters whose delusions keep their rubber knees from flexing until they either trip on their own toes or are fatally distracted by someone yelling from the darkness of the crowd.

The London Stock Exchange is no different from the New York version. Exhaustion is a diverting catch-all for the kinds of emotions that the Stock Exchange would like us to think are no more a part of share investment than they are of exploratory surgery or conveyancing. The last thing Sir Nicholas Goodison wants us to suspect is that Stock Markets are petulant, greedy, timorous and downright hysterical. Yet awful things happen in much the same way that they happen at riotous football matches or demonstrations. The difference is that the provocation for the Stock Market riot doesn't come from a Milwall gang, but from inside the collective consciousness. (Retrogrades like to characterize the psychology of a crowd of men as being identical to that of a single woman.) There was no meaning to what was going on – just as the Great Crash of 1929 had fuelled its own progress by ignorance, by the same helplessness in the face of events. 'There was no meaning'. How terrible *that* sounds, when you compare it with the rational objectives that the Stock Market habitually claims: We're here to raise money for companies. We provide a source of reliable gain for pension funds and life assurance schemes. We are a responsible outlet for the speculative ambitions of the rich and the merely well-to-do. And, yes, we tend, from time to time, to suffer a seizure, a breakdown of such proportions that in the space of a few hours, no longer than it takes to roast a joint of beef or drive from London to Oxford, your investments can shed millions and millions of pounds.

The world markets picked themselves up before collapsing a little further. On Tuesday, the London Stock Market managed a 19 point rise, and the authorities in Hong Kong raised their provision to support the broken futures market with an extra HK$2bn. Then, on Wednesday, the FOOTSIE dropped back 44, to 1658.4. By this time, a certain grimness had set in. Some said that on the first few days of the crash, broking firms were taking it without too much discomfort. 'The dealers were still laughing, joking, throwing darts around in the quiet patches . . . It wasn't like the papers said at all. It wasn't full of grown men, weeping,' confided a broker from a big multinational hybrid. By the middle of the second week, though, too many people had begun to dwell on the possibilities that waited for them once the market decayed too far. There is a clear distinction between a readjustment or a shake-out – something brisk, energetic and purgative – and a collapse which leaves your turnover at nothing, your profits threatened and your job as an analyst, a dealer, a chartist, markedly underfunded.

A fresh suspension of disbelief picked the market up on Thursday. It took back 23.6 points; while Friday saw it go up another 67.8, to close on the week at 1749.8. Your tottering Jaguar shares were still badly off though. Thursday the 29th saw then down to 301. That's from 508 two weeks earlier. Nearly half the value of your shares gone to crash hysteria. Nevertheless, by Friday, they were up to 329. Clearly, the market had thought of something.

After a fortnight or so of chaos, Wall Street and the City (and Tokyo, Hong Kong, Frankfurt and so on) had decided what it was that was wrecking their markets. It was the US budget deficit and the US trade deficit. But everyone knew this already. Yes, but the added intellectual component was that the Bull Market had become a rabble of Bear selling because sentiment had changed. This begged a desperate question: *why* had sentiment changed? No one had any very clear reasons as to why sentiment had changed just when it did, but that wasn't important. The thing was to lay down any pretence about the seriousness of the market place, confess to your jabbering emotionalism, and look for something to *change your sentiment back again*. Someone important had to say something convincing, something that most investors and professionals could place some confidence in. A psychological reconstruction was needed.

The wrong things to say were the kind of jeremiads that the US Treasury Secretary, James Baker came out with on the brink of the crash. The Germans had tightened up their economy, rather than relaxing it, as they'd promised at the Louvre finance ministers' meeting earlier in the year. This was not what the US needed to keep its appetites fed. Baker complained that the German bankers shouldn't expect the Great Glutton to put up with it; it wasn't 'in keeping with the spirit of what we agreed to as recently as earlier this month in Washington . . .' So the Germans retorted that it was not 'very helpful that Mr Baker used a lower dollar as a threat or weapon against other nations . . .' If the Americans, the Germans went on puritannically, 'don't change the pattern of consumer spending, they'll continue to have trade deficits.'

The right things to say, supposedly, were 'the underlying econ-

omy remains sound', as a White House spokesman feebly insisted at
the start of the crash. It was also a good idea to let it be known that
President Reagan's mind had been steered towards the contemplation
of a number of budget reforms, sponsored by the Republicans in
Congress. It got to the point where another White House spokesman
emerged with this gem of futile optimism. Reagan, he said, had 'a
very useful working session'. Significantly, 'they got down to
looking at numbers and what they mean, and at specific proposals
and how they may work . . .' You can hear the gathering panic in
every phrase, every desperate abstraction – 'looking at numbers and
what they mean – and how they may work . . .'

Later on, Nigel Lawson, the Chancellor of the Exchequer, confirmed to the House of Commons, that 'the strength of the British
economy, and of the public finances, puts us in the best possible
position to weather any storm'. A day later, he made a speech at the
Mansion House, where he came out with some more emollient.
'Industry,' he said, 'should have no terror of the present squall. Now
is the time to look beyond the turbulence of the markets, and invest
for growth.' This was from the man who a week or so earlier had
been scorning the City's 'grotesque overreaction' to Wall Street's
breakdown. Now, the time was right, he thought, to gesture to the
good things of life. The British economy was not 'something which
will be blown away by a financial blizzard, however violent it may
seem at the time'.

Lawson was not alone. Indeed, a murmur of nervy cheer had
been trying to make its way round the world ever since Black
Monday. The same formulations were passed round in an effort to
stanch the crash. 'The stability today was very welcome.' 'I think we
are in for a calmer week on the market.' 'There's some tremendous
value out there.'

It had to be done. The confidence trick had fallen apart. The City
had to build a new one, somehow. The City professionals, smarting
with shame at what was happening to their reputations, owed it to
their investors, to industry, to the market as a whole, to the economy. But they had the ghost of Galbraith looming over their
shoulders all the time.

The ghost of Galbraith lived in J. K. Galbraith's *The Great Crash*

1929, which he wrote in 1954 as an antidote to writer's block encountered while producing *The Affluent Society*. In his introduction, he describes how much he enjoyed taking time out in the Baker Library at Dartmouth College to work on his *Crash* manuscript; how the summer of 1954 was richly beautiful; even how the Hanover Inn (hard by the library) served a Martini and a good meal, when he'd done enough for one day. You'd expect the book, as a consequence, to be expansive, generous, relaxed in tone. In fact, it's more like a bulletin from a Yankee Tacitus. It's so astringent, so unexpectedly funny, that it became one of his outright best sellers. At the time of our Great Crash, Penguin Books held the paperback rights, and had a current edition available. They sold out. They had to rush into print again to cope with the demand. Everyone was either reading Galbraith or quoting him. But Galbraith's book didn't intrude just because of its Attic style and its disdain of human vanity. What made it haunting was that while it described the crash of 1929, it could also have been a forecast for the crash of 1987. Things had changed in sixty years, but not as much as one might have hoped. And when Galbraith got onto his memorable pillorying of Doctor Julius Klein and his express belief in the 'fundamental soundness of [the] great mass of economic activities', and Waddill Catchings' assertion that business conditions were 'unquestionably fundamentally sound', and John D. Rockefeller's revelation that 'believing that fundamental conditions of the country are sound . . . my son and I have for some days been purchasing sound comon stocks', all of which was said shortly before the market began its steady fall to the point where it lost some 90 per cent of its value, then people couldn't help but compare the latter-day Doctor Julius Kleins with their forebear.

'The underlying economy remains sound', said the White House spokesman. Variations on this theme came up over and over again, particularly from City commentators and analysts. The strength of the British economy, Lawson insisted, 'puts us in the best possible position to weather any storm.' The chairman of Warburgs was quoted as saying, 'We are in a more resilient position economically and politically than we have been for some time.' President Ronald Reagan, after the dollar had fallen to $1.80 against the pound, said,

'We are not doing anything to bring it down. I don't look for a further decline. I don't want a further decline.' He also went for goal with this one: 'Everyone is a little puzzled. There is nothing wrong with the economy.' And then scored: 'The economy,' he said, 'is strong and fundamentally sound.' Chancellor Nigel Lawson, again, remarked that any general anxieties about a big world recession were 'grossly exaggerated'. And so on. Yet, even as one pundit after another opened his mouth to deliver a bullish, the-worst-is-behind-us, the underlying economy remains sound, bromide, the ghost of Galbraith peered over his shoulder. You had to say these things; but everyone knew that they were merely things to say.

On the third week of the crash, the FOOTSIE lost another 129 points, to stand at 1620.8. There was more exhaustion about, and instead of panic at what might happen, there was a growing intimacy with what had happened. The Americans, it was being suggested, had fouled their own stock market particularly badly, by relying on a couple of computer tricks to run trades during the crash.

One was a straightforward trigger device which automatically started to sell stocks once they'd hit a predetermined low price, a neat imitation of dealer hysteria which filled in any opportunities to panic which the manual traders had missed. The other was an excessively clever use of futures trading to insure the value of a share portfolio. If the price of shares is falling, portfolio insurers sell futures contracts in Chicago, on the shares themselves, that will guarantee a buyer at their present price. Masses of sell orders, in a crash, happen at the same time. The pressure of selling on the Chicago futures market causes it to fall by 20 points. This sets off more heavy selling on Wall Street. The computers fix it all up in an unbroken descending spiral. New York's Salomon Brothers alone managed to put over $600m into stock index futures in the first hour of trading on Black Monday. They were *investing* in a stock market collapse.

Was anyone else to blame? Young traders had done badly. Old-style jobbers used to be more cautious, more leery about the way they dealt with price changes on the market because they were in partnerships and it was their money that suffered. But not these young, anarchic traders. It was August all over again.

There was also a certain amount of dread felt about the private investor. The private investor wasn't so much an instigator of the crash, as a piece of wreckage left behind after the first bad weeks. A firm of stockbrokers called A. J. Bekhor ('the small investor is particularly welcomed and catered for,' they crooned in their ad. at the back of *An Introduction To The Stock Market*) arranged for an £80m banking facility just in case settlement day, which comes roughly every sixteen days, arrived and no one was able to meet their bills. A representative of Bekhor, a firm called Manny Marks, had thirty-eight clients on its books who between them were liable for £5m of losses on the traded options market.

DEBRIS

But Settlement Day (2 November) came and went, and no one threw themselves from a high building. The Dow Jones Index started to go up again.

All the same there were some victims, after the worst events had passed. It was hard to feel very sorry for the most visible ones. In the first week of the crash, as the papers were keen to tell us, Rupert Murdoch had lost £487m of his personal fortune; Sir Terence Conran was down by £23m; while the Fortes (of Trust House Forte) had lost £37m. ICI had shed £2.716bn, while British Telecom were out by £1.98bn. And prices were still falling. But they'd make it up, eventually.

This was not the case with an Australian plutocrat, with the refreshingly antique name of Robert Holmes à Court. He was famous at the time for being a millionaire alternative to Rupert Murdoch. While Murdoch, with his intimidating stare, his eyebrows and his habit of consuming anyone who got in his way, symbolized one kind of Australian entrepreneurial philosophy, Robert Holmes à Court habitually received a different press. He was 'the chess player – the coolest man in town – the Melbourne marksman – the Sydney sharpshooter. Like Robert Maxwell, or Sir James Goldsmith, Robert Holmes à Court could make things happen just by letting you know that he was thinking of making things happen. He gazed out of the financial papers with a look of slightly weary amusement. He had large, doleful eyes and very big ears, like an animal of the forest. He always looked trim, conservative, resistlessly calculating. His personal wealth was put somewhere at £545m. He owned an island off Queensland, an £8m Regency mansion in Regents Park, two stud farms and a collection of vintage cars. By mid-November the markets had caught him.

In the first couple of weeks of the crash, the Australian Stock Market lost about A$75bn, or £35bn. Holmes à Court's own holdings (in a Monopoly-board of different companies) lost around A$2bn. Shares in the Bell Group, the capstone in the Holmes à Court enterprise, fell from A$10.60 to A$2.90. The price of Bell Resources, a limb of the Bell Group, went from A$6.40 to A$1.50. Other plutocrats who owned large amounts of shares in themselves or in other companies were in the same kind of position, but there was a difference in Holmes à Court's case; more than most he had used his shareholdings as collateral against which to borrow very large sums of money. He was highly geared – this is what you are when you borrow very large sums of money against your equity. Once the worth of the collateral had violently collapsed, Holmes à Court had no security. The banks were toying with the idea of calling in their loans. The 'coolest man in town' was left staring at various unsavoury ways of raising the cash to service his borrowings. He was going to have to sell himself to the world.

On the other side of the world, there was more disastrous gearing, but this was as nothing in comparison with Robert Holmes à Court and his £3bn multinational. It involved Anil Gupta. Anil Gupta was a 23-year-old trainee accountant who lived in west London. He geared himself up on the traded options market around the time of the crash, and when the crash had settled, found that he owed his brokers, County NatWest over £1m. Now to avoid the possibility of a speculator telephoning a broker to trade in the options market and then defaulting on his payments at the end of the trading period, the Stock Exchange has various rules about collateral requirements and margins. This way, the brokers don't lose, and bankrupt madmen are discouraged from attempting to trade in the first place. Hypothetically, someone who wanted to trade in options based on the

FOOTSIE, might have to put up a margin of over £50,000 before taking a substantial position. Of course, this £50,000 doesn't have to be in the form of banknotes. It could be held in gilts or in a guarantee from your bank or in shares.

Gupta had none of these things, but he still managed to trade on the options market through his brokers at County NatWest. He asked for credit, and the brokers he was dealing with said, okay, you can have the credit. After a few weeks, the market had crashed by 600 points and Gupta owed County NatWest around £1m. He couldn't have chosen a more up-to-date way to go broke. Better than losing his money on the shares themselves, he lost it in *the* financial growth area of the 1980s. He did it in the modern fashion. He geared himself up on the options market. 'It makes us look so *silly*,' a County NatWest person said. When they found out what had been going on in their traded options department, they fired the three executives involved and placed a £1m writ on Gupta 'to protect our interest,' even though, they complained, 'The guy hasn't got a bean, and obviously can't pay.'

They weren't the only ones to come apart like this. A firm of stockbrokers in Wolverhampton allowed a fifteen-year-old schoolboy to buy £100,000 of shares. He was a fifth-former from Matlock and pretended to be a nineteen-year-old businessman, using phrases he had picked up in his economics lessons. One of the stockbrokers involved admitted that 'when a new customer opens an account, there has to be a certain amount of goodwill on both sides'. The goodwill ran out by the time the underage investor had gone £20,000 into debt. 'It's just one of the problems of wider share ownership,' said the stockbrokers.

Meanwhile, in Dublin a dealer working for the giant Citicorp, the second largest bank in the States, managed to lose some £25m on his own unauthorized deals. He panicked on Black Monday, started trading wildly with $100m of Citicorps money, and lost. The deals were never recorded on the bank's books, and only came to light some nine days later when the confirmations started to come in from other broking firms.

The controls broke down, they all said. People got credit, they got margin, they geared themselves up and they exceeded their dealing limits. And these were the ones who got caught. While Robert Holmes à Court could look down on a collapsing empire and still be rich by the time it had collapsed, these people had thrown everything away on speculations which Holmes à Court wouldn't even have thought worth the effort. But there they were, geared up and borrowed up to the neck, all appealing to the crash and the terrible indexes to go up and let them live again. Their personal chaos was a testimonial to the drawing power of the revolutionized new City.

The prudent father with his life insurance and his private pension scheme; the retired couple with a little unit trust that was maturing nicely in September and worth a quarter less by October; people with company pension schemes; people working for companies who fed the Great Glutton when it was hungry (and which was now contemplating a diet, and would no longer require quite so many delicacies); Lucky Paul's father who glumly resigned his portfolio to another three years of trudging towards profitability: millions lost millions in the crash of 1987. Only the Ace Merchant Banker, who panicked after the August slump, didn't suffer. He had about £75,000 in mixed equities and gilts. He sold off the equities, and put the proceeds into fixed interest investments. The NatWest's high interest deposit account came into fleeting fashion that month.

Webb tore through more packets of Silk Cut than usual in those weeks, while he mooed encouragements and solicitudes down the phone to his clients. Lucky Paul fed him a line of patter about fundamental soundness and underlying stability, even while the market was uniformly red. Things were readjusting. Things were correcting. That made it sound better. And by November, Lucky Paul, Webb, the whole multinational stockbroking combine could say in a new verse to the company song, that the Index was merely back to its position of last November. Forget about the twelve months you've just lived through! They shouldn't have happened, anyway. The market was overvalued; it was a necessary correction. The whole year was really one big aberration. Reagan's mind is now at home with the concept of a $76bn package of sincerely non-cosmetic budget deficit cuts; the fundamental economy is sound. There may be a temporary recession, but not a *depression*, no sir! Put down that Galbraith!

146

The best thing to do, was to sit it out and *not* to invest in the BP share issue. That was law. The BP share issue was a Government privatization which had missed its entry and was not, for once, going to turn into magic money.

The Government and its adviser, bankers N. M. Rothschild, had set the offer at 330p a share, with 2.194bn shares up for purchase. This was the remaining 31.5 per cent holding that Government had in the company. The rest of BP's shares were already available on the Stock Market, just like any other company shares. But the price of 330p, just like the British Gas, British Telecom, Jaguar share issues, was pitched low, so as to pull in as many buyers as possible, thus broadening the evangelical popular capitalism movement. The total revenue for the Government was due to be £7.2bn. The PR team for this one, had a group of Royal Marines abseil down the side of the 32-storey BP headquarters in London, tearing a piece of cloth away from the enormous numbers hidden underneath. Significantly, one of them get stuck about half-way down. He had to struggle with his ropes and shackles and PR gimmicks before the cloth came away and he could carry on down the side of the very large building. Then, it seemed funny.

And there they were, the biggest numbers you could imagine, reading 330. Everyone stared witlessly at these things for a while, and then went on their way. Immediately after the price announcement, the crash happened. The biggest Government privatization, the privatization to end all privatizations, was knocked out. Because the greater part of BP's shares were already being traded on the Stock Market, there was a gradual rupture between the current going price and the 330p set for the privatization shares. Eventually, BP was being traded at 266p, a whole 64p less than what the Government expected people to pay for the privatization issue.

The underwriters, the banks who agree to take all the shares even if no-one wants them, made a genteel spectacle of themselves. There were seventeen British banks and seven American and Canadian firms acting as underwriters. The first thing they did was insist that the Chancellor of the Exchequer cancel the offer. If he didn't, they were going to have to pay for these shares at 330p and then try to sell them on the open market. They were going to lose a lot of money, the Americans especially. Whereas the British banks had sub-underwritten their exposure among another 450 institutions, the Americans (Goldman Sachs, Morgan Stanley, Salomon Brothers and Shearson Lehman) hadn't arranged any sub-underwriting and were liable for the whole sum: 126m BP shares each, with a paper loss for each bank of £80m. Even James Baker, the US Treasury Secretary, intervened and told Lawson to give up. It was bizarrely satisfying to note these very rich institutions (who'd made a healthy fortune out of underwriting fees on other, safer, privatizations) fretting at the prospect of having to do what they'd undertaken to do.

Lawson nevertheless went for the issue, but with a guaranteed buy-back arrangement to sustain confidence in the scheme. This was a notion that Warburgs had thought up. The Bank of England would buy back any unwanted shares from people who'd committed to purchase them if the price of the part-paid shares went below 70p. It seemed like a good idea. The part-paid shares, for which some people had actually paid 120p, started trading at 86p.

And yet, once again, it revealed the world of difference that lay between those at the top and the scurrying nobodies at the bottom of the financial heap. Just as Robert Holmes à Court's worries centered on how much of his billionaire status he was going to keep, while Gupta and the rest worried about how they were going to *exist*, so the BP issue lit up the perspectives of the big institutions – how do we avoid this dross? – and the small investor – why isn't this one working like the others?

Lucky Paul's mother, and hundreds like her, got into trouble. She'd become keen after the famous British Airways sale and Lucky Paul's father's shares with their magical added worth. She looked for a long time at the great application form in the *Telegraph*, with its fuddling 'Terms and Conditions' ('. . . agree that time of payment by you shall be of the essence of each contract constituted by acceptance of your application . . . If you write "yes" in Box 4 of a public application form . . . you will not be entitled to exercise any remedy of rescission . . .'), its declarations, 'WARNING', Box 2, Joint Applicants, N. M. Rothschild & Sons Limited, and then asked her husband for some help in completing it. He laughed at her, then realized that she meant it.

Lucky Paul's father called Lucky Paul. Lucky Paul spent a tumultuous half hour on the phone, urging his mother back into line. He explained to her that if she wanted BP shares more than she wanted anything else in the world, he could buy them for 45p less than she was ready to pay now. They were the same shares in the same company, but cheaper. Not that anyone was buying at the time, because prices were still falling fast. Three months' time, maybe. Couldn't she *wait*? And she came back with an increasingly untidy rationale involving the security of a large company and the double security of the Government's involvement, and even if they weren't worth so much now, they *would* be worth 330p eventually, and then they might be worth more than that and she'd *heard* of BP, and bought her petrol from one of their garages and knew perfectly well that they were the kind of company that wasn't going out of business, in fact it was like her grandmother's old railway shares, quite safe, no reason at all not to invest in them . . .

Lucky Paul marshalled his hysteria. He made her an offer. He said, 'Don't worry about filling in the application form (terribly fiddly, I can't understand half of it myself) just send me the money and I'll buy the shares for you.' She struggled with this for a while. It had been her idea, after all. She was going to do this thing. But she now had some formless, brooding doubts about the issue, something to do with the price being lower or higher – or not worth so much. She gave in. She wrote out a cheque for £2000 and sent it to Lucky Paul who put it straight into the NatWest high interest deposit account.

And yet, on the television, on the last day for applications, there were still muttering, helpless investors coming to the front door of the bank and handing in their completed applications. The TV reporter standing outside went up to them. 'Why are you doing this?' he'd ask. 'Don't you know you can buy the shares cheaper?' A woman backed away from him after she'd just committed, what? Her life savings? Her entire pension? She said, 'I don't know – I don't know'. Something drove these poor people on into the bank, to place their orders and pay their money. Some mangled understanding of the privatization gift and the joy of stagging must have rooted in their minds, where it became a fixed belief, an article of trust, that privatizations were always good.

The confidence trick had failed. The *Annus Mirabilis* had come to an end, within a week of the full year. It had been a modern crash. It had depended on the instancy of the £4bn electronic market. It had preyed on the nerves of the young traders. It had worked itself up through the anonymity of screen dealing. It had simultaneously wrecked a privatization, and blighted the dream of popular capitalism. It was the right sort of crash for the modern City.

9

WINTER 1987: THE SPIRIT OF OCTOBER

You had the feeling, watching the City in the last quarter of 1987, that events were all connected at some deep level, that someone or something was trying to make a point. Was there an infernal strategy, a spirit of October?

MORE GUINNESS

Even as the crash was approaching the sleeping City, a group of very rich men was wondering about what jail might look like from the inside. These were the men of the Guinness arrests. Saunders had already been charged back in May. But the Fraud Squad (under the leadership of Detective Superintendent Botwright) had been toiling away on the case, and by mid-October, they were ready to place some more accusations before him.

So, on Tuesday 13 October, Saunders entered Bow Street Magistrates' Court to face no less than thirty-seven fresh criminal charges. Among them was a charge of theft, involving around £25m: the sum which, it was agreed, had been used to inflate the price of Guinness shares during the Distillers takeover. He took the opportunity to hold a press conference in the Waldorf Hotel. He told the newsmen, 'Not a day passes without messages of support. This is one of the things that has stopped my family from reaching the deep realms of depression . . .' Investors with a few Guinness shares to their names would come up to him on the Underground, to which he was now reduced, and proffer their sympathy. 'I have had to sell my house to pay legal fees. I have no income at all. I did not receive a Halpernese-type salary,' (Sir Ralph Halpern and his £1m

plus annual wage, being the benchmark for all modern businessmen)
'I started at Guinness on £60,000 a year. You are not able to make
many savings on that . . .'

Gerald Ronson, on the other hand, was a different kind of person
altogether. Ronson had tried to preempt the Fraud Squad by paying
back his support fee, and making a formal apology. It didn't work.
He went round to the Fraud Squad offices for a discussion, and
found himself charged with eight criminal offences. One of these
was startlingly arcane – conspiracy to create a false market in
shares. This is a common law offence, which had been more or less
untouched since the late nineteenth century. The most celebrated
example goes back further than that, and occurs in R. v de Berenger,
where the defendants were charged with conspiring to raise the
price of government funds. They had gone about spreading a rumour
that Napoleon Bonaparte was dead and that the King would make
peace with the French people. This was their way of doing a little
illicit ramping. The Fraud Squad were evidently working hard to
nail their victims down at every point.

Yet it was the sight of Ronson himself which made it so gripping.
Saunders looked like a wrecked businessman. His life was falling
apart; but Ronson was impervious. He looked like a tycoon. There
was something inexplicable about his expensive tie, and the way it
was knotted, and the set of his shirt-collar, and above all, his *hair*
with a parting as decisive and straight as a gun barrel. Saunders' hair
was thin to begin with, and was, by October, listless and depressed
– average, downtrodden human hair. But Ronson's hair with its
packed solidity and mineral sheen, was armoured. Indeed, the whole
of Ronson appeared to be armoured. The press footled around with
words like stocky and powerful, to describe his appearance. Really,
he looked short and incredibly tough. An arrest just seemed to
bounce off him. This and the hair, and the little manifestations of
other priorities, other wealth, suggested that tycoons really were a
different species.

This was confirmed by Sir Jack Lyons, a senior statesman in City
terms. He also had been arrested, and charged with theft, involving
more than £3m. This, supposedly, was another part of the £25m
involved in the takeover. Lyons admitted to receiving at least some

152

of the money, but argued that it was legitimate payment for services rendered, in particular, lobbying against a referral to the MMC. Still there he was, walking into Bow Street as well, wearing an impossibly expensive shirt and tie and a dark, tycoon's suit, and looking quite unlike the common crowd. It didn't seem to bother him. This was a man who, after all, was tycoon enough to invite the Prime Minister to lunch.

And then, on Friday the 16th, the day of the Hurricane, Roger Seelig, the Tudor Courtier, arrived at Bow Street to hear twelve charges, including one of theft of around £3m of Guinness's money.

It was as if each one had been chosen for his symbolic impact. There was the dynamic Ronson with his armoured hair, and his billion-pound private company. There was Sir Jack Lyons, seventy-one at the time of his arrest, authoritatively senior (Chairman of the Sir Jack Lyons Charitable Trust ... Vice-President of the Anglo-Italian Chamber of Commerce). There was Saunders, the top employee, the lupine, obsessive, business expeditor. There was Seelig, the youthful banker who moved like a diplomat among these people. They were, it seemed, the absolute nonpareils of the business and finance worlds. And yet, within days of each other, they'd fallen to Botwright.

REDUNDANCY

A couple of days after Seelig had been let out on bail (£500,000, the same as for the others) the crash came to obscure the unease at the Guinness arrests. And then, once the shock had started to die down, people began to lose their jobs. The timing was eerie. The simple-minded concluded that they were losing their jobs because of the crash, but in fact they were marked for redundancy before the crash came.

Back in September, Shearson Lehman Brothers International, the gargantuan US investment bank, looked at the findings of an internal operating review and decided to fire some of their staff. The redundancies were in the equities business it acquired when they bought up the British stockbrokers L. Messel. It meant that 150 people had to go, weeks before the crash happened, before redundancies became anything like part of the currency of City language.

At the same time, Salomon Brothers, another American investment bank were thinking about their own internal review. They set up fifteen separate investigatory units to look into the bank's various operations. For four weeks, starting early in September, the investigatory units would each appear in turn before the bank's board to deliver a lecture based on their findings. These lectures, and the discussions that followed, would run from 1.30 p.m. to 7.00 p.m. Then the board would wait for the next investigatory unit to report the next day. Finally, they drew up a list of recommendations, which they passed on to the Chairman, John Gutfreund, and the President and the Vice-Chairman. Gutfreund went along with the recommendations, and ordered a straight 12 per cent cut in staff.

Now, by this time Salomon Brothers were a very big institution indeed. They had tripled in size between 1982 and 1987. They employed some 6500 people. They had built themselves the biggest dealing floor in the world, in a preposterous new office block near Victoria railway station. They acquired no less than 40 per cent of their staff in one year alone, 1986. They had the kind of overweening massiveness that people inside such a company take as a guarantee of their basic security and which those outside see as a symptom of imperial decline. They were going to be *the* global securities house. They were already the kings of US bond trading. They underwrote one fifth of all US debt and equity issues. What they weren't so good at, though, was the purer business of merchant banking, the business in which you make money through your professional expertise, rather than your trading power. And when the US bond market collapsed earlier in 1987, they lost some $100m while still having to find the money for all their 6500 employees, and still having to fund their imperial palace in Victoria. So they decided to sack 800 people – 650 from New York; 150 in London.

Some people had been looking askance at the Americans ever since their arrival in London to corner the Eurobond market. In the early 1980s British firms had complained that the Americans, vor-

aciously buying up talent for the Big Bang, had soured it for everyone else. They were the people who invented the £20,000 starting
incomes and terrific financial inducements. They were possessed by
the idea of being the biggest, giving the total financial in-house
service. They were going to sell any client anything he wanted,
with great mountains of Yankee wealth to back it up. They were
going to hire the best people in town, and the best people in town
(the Yankees concluded) will go to whoever offers them a fortune
first. They had made things quite unpleasant.

So, as the obverse of their blockheaded approach to hiring people
they revealed themselves to be the worst at sacking them – or at
least, they started a trend of incompetent and mismanaged sackings
which wound through the City month after month, and which was
always most closely associated with the Americans. In Salomon's
case, you can see how the myth of the World's Least Sympathetic
Humans took root.

Once John Gutfreund and his team had made up their minds to
fire 150 staff from the London operation, someone in the firm told
the press. They didn't tell the staff, they told the *press*. The *Financial
Times* for Monday 12 October ran a story about half-way through
the newspaper on Salomon's various troubles. 'Salomon's, which is
struggling to manage the impact of rapid growth in its trading
operations, confirmed at the weekend that it would today announce
some conclusions of a large-scale "strategic review" . . .' On Tuesday
13 October, the headline on page one of the *Financial Times*, read:
'Salomon Brothers Cuts Staff And Trading Operations'. The story
underneath went on, 'In a bleak confirmation of its problems,
Salomon said that the parent group was only "marginally" profitable
in the third quarter to September, after earnings collapsed from
$117m to $40m in the June quarter . . .' And then it announced the
12 per cent staff reduction, to help cut the business's overheads by
$150m a year.

Now imagine yourself, a virgin from university, with all the
money and ambitions that went with your job, picking up the *FT* on
the Tuesday morning and seeing *that*.

One of the victims sat back (at eleven in the morning, a time of
day for housewives, writers and people without a job) and said,

'First they had a recruitment freeze; then another recruitment freeze. Then the management had a meeting to allay fears about staff cuts, which made us more suspicious, then they leaked it to the press first, so no-one did much work for a week. And they didn't tell us till *Friday*.'

A week of terrified inaction passed. People worried about their cheap mortgages, company cars, medical insurances, the money they'd spent on the strength of the bonuses they hadn't yet received. Some of them could remember the bustling prose in the Salomon's recruitment material: 'The rewards of a career at Salomon Brothers reach beyond the successfully completed merger transaction, the annual underwriting championship, the new product idea or even the year-end bonus ... Salomon Brothers takes great pride in its ability to hire and train the brightest and most motivated people from a broad spectrum of cultural and environmental backgrounds. Each professional learns that he or she is first of all a member of Salomon Brothers.' Then they were sacked. 'We just sat there, waiting for the phone to ring.' The former Salomon's employee looked around his home, balefully. 'One by one, a phone would ring, and someone would get up and go into the office, and come out with an envelope. They handled it pretty insensitively. Everybody got the same word processed letter. Half the people burst into tears ...'

He didn't burst into tears in the office, but three weeks later (in his part-paid house, with the floorboards poking out beyond the fringes of a giveaway carpet) he had time to dwell on Salomon's shoddiness. 'They take a trader's view. They take on staff on the basis of a good quarter's figures; or if they're bad, they'll lay some more off.' He was not optimistic at the prospect of getting a new job. By this time, the crash had happened and everyone knew that business was going to be worse before it got better. 'Of all the people I know who were fired from Salomon's I don't know anyone who's got a job. I've written to about twenty places and got three interviews.'

After Shearson Lehman and Salomon had dismissed their staff, it seemed that everyone was entertaining the idea. Chemical Bank (another US banking concern, also known as Comical Bank, on account of some past deals) decided to lose 170 of its 950 London employees. At around this time a City Folk myth emerged which said that one bank had abruptly sacked one of their young tyros and thrown him out of his office. The tyro, the story insists, took his company Porsche, drove it up to the front doors of the building, parked it across them in such a way that no one could get in or out, set the car's burglar alarm off and walked away, throwing the car keys down a storm grating as he did so.

The rest of the City started to yield. By the 30 November, the *Evening Standard* felt certain enough of its facts to yelp: 'Bang Go 10,000 City Jobs.' This was a highly speculative extrapolation of a trend. An intelligent observer was quoted as saying that the figure 'wasn't impossible', and it certainly created a little more anxiety. Orion Bank dropped 150 jobs. Market turnover by early 1988 was standing at no more than £800m a day, compared with £3bn a year earlier. The crash meant that trading firms who'd depended on the turnover of stock during the Bull market to make a living were stuck. After the crash, trading volumes had collapsed, and if you were still living off the touch then your profits were vanishing.

Merrill Lynch was set to fire 150 from their London offices; Citicorp said that around 100 had to go; L. F. Rothschild, more Americans, sacked 50; Manufacturers Hanover was casting around to fire 2500 of its staff, worldwide; Greenwell Montagu, the Midland bank's crushed stockbroking firm, gave up trying to be an equity broking outfit at all, and decided to give all its attention to the gilts market. This meant that 230 jobs in the equities division had to go.

County NatWest sacked 165 members of staff, once it had taken over the stockbrokers Wood Mackenzie. There were suddenly too many people doing the same job in the same building. Head office demanded a rethink. In a bid to wrest the laurel of The World's Least Sympathetic Humans from the Americans, the senior managers waited until Friday – so that the victims had all weekend to think about it – and then called them in one by one. Brokers were, apparently, asked to wait at their desks until they were called. They were requested to take their personal effects with them when they finally saw their department heads. Their department heads told them that their services were no longer needed. They were then sent to the personnel department, where a maggot handed them a manilla envelope and told them to leave the building immediately. Could you conceive of this? (the City Old Boy fulminates.) Could you imagine this happening in a proper firm? Maggots in personnel who give you your cards, like a back office junior? These men made *millions*, some of them, and you give them a *manilla envelope*?

There was a rumour that some of the sacked ones were so outraged at the way they were being treated, they smashed up their TV screens in the battery pen. You can see how the months of boredom and terror and sweatiness and animalism, balled up in the stomachs of the men at the TV screens, might have at last overwhelmed the sacked ones, and driven them into long dreamt of acts of violence.

'I've just drunk two bottles of wine,' a redundant Eurobond dealer muttered over the telephone. 'I'm going to drink another one. Went to Paris for the weekend to try and cheer myself up. It didn't work – made things worse in fact. Had another job interview. I don't know what I'm going to do.'

The headlines kept up a note of thrilled horror, all this time. 'City Axe Keeps On Swinging', they announced. 'Redundancy Fears Mount In The City'. 'City Casualties Rise'. Webb looks on it all with disdain. The point that the clever young men and women have missed, he explains, is that your job is not just about gambling; it is a gamble itself, no less than taking a position on 5m Amalgamated Consolidated shares. The job comes and goes. They pay you a lot, they sack you. 'These kids think it's a load of money *and* a job for life. They shouldn't be here, if that's what they think.' You can hardly blame them for being shocked though. The inducements to come into the City in the first place argued its solid, expansionist professionalism, not its aptitude for collapsing in a week. 'We aim to be in among the top players; this is a long-term commitment. We aim to build, using the best talent, wherever it comes from.' And so on. You'd have to be a hard case, a Webb at the age of twenty-four, if you could ignore that and merely live day-to-day.

The Big Bang was founded on two mutually exclusive propositions: we are all going to get big and powerful for the new age, and will ensure our future by doing so; but we all know, everybody knows, that there isn't going to be enough room for everyone, and some people are going to suffer. The crash wasn't a necessary product of Big Bang, although it was characterized by it; but shrinkage and retrenchment were built into the Big Bang right from the start. It had to happen, but you couldn't allow yourself to think that it would happen in such a way that you would be hurt by it. The suspension of disbelief which sustained the Bull Market is an echo of the contradiction at the centre of Big Bang.

'That's what it means to work in the City,' Webb barks. 'If you can't take the uncertainties you shouldn't be here.' Lucky Paul acknowledges this truth, although it depresses him. Where's the solidity of the professions? he wonders. Why is the whole thing run with the contingency of a gang of road layers?

And, along with many others, Lucky Paul and Webb started to notice that one or two people who used to be around weren't any more, When County NatWest or Salomon's made a big thing of it and lost 150 jobs, you knew where you were. But elsewhere, there were tiny killings going on all the time. 'People just don't turn up for work any more. One day they're there; the next, they're not. Two or three just disappear each week,' murmured a banker from one of the great new financial combines. Then what do they do? A City headhunter squinted at the problem. 'It's not so bad for the young ones. They've got degrees, they're single, no attachments, they can work somewhere else. But,' she said, with a note of genuine pain, 'the thirty-five-year-old, the forty-year-old, three children, mortgage, car, no degree. Where does *he* go? The ones who came in before it all got very ritzy – the ones who were okay at their job, nothing special, but were kept on because they fitted in – they've got no futures, really.' Webb thought that they went and ran mini-cab companies. 'The job is the gamble.' The Ace Merchant Banker hardly notices the crash, busy as he is with loan restructuring. Keith the Computer Demon is too valuable – more valuable than ever – to his firm, as he slaves away at quicker reaction times for the software and new ways of processing the back office work. And Webb? Fortyish, kids, debts, dependencies? Webb doesn't allow himself to think of it.

*

The *Annus Mirabilis* was over, and the spirit of October was settling in. Why, even the City Airport went down with it.

At the time, the City Airport was a little short-hop aerodrome, built in among the new Docklands developments, and intended for City workers and docklands *arrivistes*. From it, you could take a businessman's shuttle to Paris, Brussels and Southampton. Until, that is, Friday, 18 December when the Civil Aviation Authority suspended flights to Paris from the airport after pilots started complaining of near misses. Brymon Airways, one of two airlines flying the route, wrote to the CAA twelve times to complain that they were likely to crash into another plane in the uncontrolled airspace between Sevenoaks and Eastbourne. The CAA capitulated and ordered an enquiry.

The fancy airport, another token of City internationalism, with its step-on, no-fuss procedures and its executive emphasis, is closed. The soaring ambitions of the City are switched off by the CAA!

It seemed as if the engine of the City was running slower and slower. After mania, depression. The payment for the vaunting ambition of 1986 was the dull winter of late 1987. There were no Christmas bonuses in 1987. The bigger trading houses were reporting losses after the crash of £20m and £40m. Executives at County NatWest had their salaries cut, by 20 per cent. The market was flat as a desert.

THE OTHER POLICE

And then, just when you were flattened, there was the Financial Services Act, 1986, the bureaucrats' revenge. The Financial Services Act had a meanness to it quite unlike redundancy or arrest. But it, too, denoted the end of the good times.

By the end of February 1988, anyone intending to perform some kind of financial service for the general public (such as investment management, broking, life insurance, banking) would have to join a new professional body with rules, ordinances, a structure of regulations to check their natural scope for making money. The City would have to give up the nudges and nods and clubbable elbow-squeezings which were traditionally the means by which one institution commended another to more proper ways.

At the head of everything, there would still be the Department of Trade and Industry. But, one tier below the DTI, there would be a new group of functionaries in the form of the Securities and Investments Board. This would oversee the various broking and investment activities that went on in the City. The Bank of England, as larded with powers as the SIB but awful in its fastness, would patrol bankers and gilts dealers. But then — and this is what infuriates the City — below these three great ruling bodies, there would be no less than five different self-regulatory organizations, as the DTI named them, in an effort to make the City think that it was still going to organize its own affairs.

If you are going to do business in the City, you must be a member of a self-regulatory organization, or SRO. So you join an SRO, you abide by its precepts, your membership of the SRO announces your probity to your customers. This is the idea. But no City person can admit the idea of an SRO without his bile rising. An SRO is a thing that will shackle you when you come to magic money from somewhere, or involve yourself in one of those areas where ethics slide from under you, or do the sorts of things that the City guys do and have always done.

Secondly, the very act of joining an SRO is unbearably complex and time-consuming, not least because you might have to join more than one. Consider this: Barclays de Zoete Wedd has to make twelve different applications to three separate SROs, so that all the various aspects of its business can be deemed to be legitimately regulated. It also has to report to the Bank of England, because it is a merchant bank and a dealer in gilts, and its mergers and acquisitions department also has to subscribe to the takeover code. Barclays Bank, the high street clearing bank which owns BZW, also has to report to the Bank of England on its own account, and (on its own account) has to make another six or so applications to another group of SROs.

And the SROs themselves are a bad dream of acronyms and intentions. There is FIMBRA, the Financial Intermediaries, Managers

161

and Brokers Regulatory Organization; there's TSA, The Securities Association; there's LAUTRO, the Life Assurance and Unit Trust Regulatory Organization; there's IMRO, the Investment Managers Regulatory Organization; there's the AFBD, the Association of Futures Brokers and Dealers. Now, a firm of stockbrokers will naturally join TSA, since they deal in securities. But then, do they also join IMRO, for investment managers, since they may well have various investment funds to manage? Or what about FIMBRA? And what if you're running a unit trust investment company? Do you join LAUTRO or IMRO? You probably apply to both, to make sure. What if you're a broker in FIMBRA and TSA and you want to get into unit trusts? Well, you have to join up with LAUTRO first, or IMRO, or . . .?

You have to show that you're 'fit and proper' to run a business; your accountants must produce reams of certification to prove that your past is clean; you have to hold the clients' money in a separate bank account, and obtain written agreements on what it is you're supposed to be doing for them; you must tell the client the scope and limitations of your business; you must have a formal procedure for dealing with complaints. It costs a fortune to apply, and another fortune to rewrite all the firm's computer programs so that they can supply the material your SRO will demand of you. And if you get something wrong, genuinely without meaning to, or you offer a service for which you're not fully registered and documented, then you may end up contravening the FSA and be sent to prison for as much as two years *and* be fined.

City types like to argue that there was coercive energy left in the existing legislation and organizations. Admittedly, these tended to be things like the Theft Act, and the DTI inquiries teams, things that were only good after the event, rather than assurances that the event wouldn't happen. But no one applied them vigorously enough. The Bank of England was still squeezing people's elbows and having quiet talks with them, while the rest of the world, or at least the legislators, wanted disciplines they could understand. The DTI was still compiling its overlong reports, and still getting nowhere. The legislation was all there, the City types swore. But now (they say) look at this idiotic FSA, one of the worst-drafted pieces of legislation ever seen.

Not only did the City hate the FSA, it tried to pretend it didn't exist, when the time came to register. A fortnight before the last day on which applications could be accepted (26 February), the SROs were worried. IMRO was expecting around 1200 firms to apply; they had actually heard from no more than 466. The AFBD had sent out 554 application packs, but only 34 had come back. Elsewhere, forms were being returned incomplete or incorrectly filled in. The City houses kept up a wall of complaint. They demanded more time to fill in the forms and get themselves in order. A couple of investment firms worked out how much it was going to cost them simply to adapt their internal computers so that they provided the right information. The smaller firm was looking at a cost of £380,000 a year, while the larger one estimated that the cost of setting up the new system would be £2m followed by another £500,000 to keep it going. The consultants Touche Ross claimed that the City as a whole was going to spend some £300m in the first year of the FSA on new computer systems.

The person they hated most was the man who was at the head of the SIB. He was called Sir Kenneth Berrill, and they hated him principally because it was his job to corral the City into the SROs but also because of who he was. He was an academic civil servant. He'd been a professional economist at first, then chief economic adviser in the Treasury at the start of the 1970s, then head of the Central Policy Review Staff up to 1980. In the eyes of the City, he was the last word in bloodless parochialism.

Berrill's face grew more and more lugubrious as the months went by and the City struggled to break free of him. He would raise his domed head and tent his eyebrows to make another pronouncement, or issue another unbrookable command, whereupon the City loosed off more invective and dragged its feet ever more offensively. Yet he wanted to carry on with the job: the SIB and its subordinate organizations were monuments to a philosophy which said that the small investor must be protected. That's what the FSA and the SIB and the SROs were about. They were a collateral branch of popular capitalism. Large investors and companies could be presumed to know their way around the City, and to be able to protect themselves against malpractice. But the small investor had to have some kind of friend, a Virgil to accompany him. That was Sir Kenneth Berrill and his SIB. It was a noble trust.

But when Berrill's contract came up for renewal, early in 1988, the DTI decided to let it lapse. As the multinationals said, whenever they wanted to sack someone, they 'de-emphazised' him. The DTI even entered the ranks of the World's Least Sympathetic Humans, when they obliged Berrill to ask if they would delay announcing his departure until he had told his own staff.

Slowly, the new year took on some kind of shape. The FOOTSIE dithered at around 1800; a year ago, it had gone through 2000 for the first time. Firm after firm announced losses or terrible profit shrinkages as a result of the crash. Jobs dwindled invisibly. It became almost impossible to deal in some of the Gamma stocks, the smallest and least interesting companies, because no one would make a market in them; they only wanted to handle the stocks that might make them a profit of some kind.

And Lucky Paul? Let's say this. Lucky Paul's immediate superior leaves to join a Japanese firm, and they give his job to Lucky Paul. So now he heads the electricals team. But he is also locked into a City unlike the one he joined five years before. There is no guaranteed bonus. His basic salary is stuck. And the atmosphere of the place is getting worse.

10

EARLY 1988: THE SUMP
OF OBSESSIONS

One of the problems with talking about the City, is that you can never be certain if you're describing the activities of a world financial centre or the plot of a Morality play. This confusion of possibilities has made the City more interesting as the years have passed. It's become one of Britain's last chances to beat the world and make money; and yet it's also a pit of iniquity. It's as new as anything outside Silicon Glen or a green field Japanese television factory; and yet it's full of reprehensible old City habits. And it mirrors that late twentieth-century feeling that life has been reduced to nothing but fearful risk management rather than the creation of a purposeful order.

US AND THEM

On the surface, the City's new self is a nexus of creativity, technology, reasoned action. Underneath, it's greed and panic. It reacts rather than rules. It's a place for the world's money to rampage through; you can't *do* anything about international finance, it seems, except herd bits of it loosely in the direction you'd like them to go. The rest is hope. And if the stock markets crash, if currencies collapse, if bond issues disintegrate and multinational companies turn out to have been run by crazed peculators, then the City can do no more than find a way of dealing with it, after the event. We want the place to work, if only because the British economy needs it so badly; but all the time, we have the feeling that the best it can do is *cope* with the Americans, the new technology it's bought itself, the attentions of the police and the politicians, the Japanese, the horrors of true competition, the scares of the money world. It was never in control, even while it was reorganizing itself throughout the 1980s. It was engaged in a self-contradiction: a reorganization that ran riot.

Various creative people capitalized on this confusion. Caryl Churchill wrote *Serious Money*; Tony Marchant wrote a play called *Speculators*; and then there was Oliver Stone's film about Ivan Boesky, *Wall Street*. *Serious Money* won awards, and drew large audiences at the Wyndhams Theatre. Michael Douglas was much approved of by Wall Street, in *Wall Street*, and won an Oscar.

Speculators, which was a fringe production in the basement of the Royal Shakespeare Company's Barbican car park, didn't get so much attention. It played to smaller audiences (the studio theatre only holds a few hundred people), it had neither the visual gimmicks nor the specially written Rap music of Caryl Churchill's play, and besides, it came long after *Serious Money*, and suffered as a consequence. But it's the more interesting of the two plays, because it exceeds people's expectations. *Serious Money*, much like *Wall Street*, works on the premise that anyone with a job in international finance is monstrously selfish and immoral. The fun comes from watching the hysteria of greed in action. In fact it is nothing but action. The cast run around shouting at each other for two whole hours. Wonderful! (the audiences agree) that's how it is! It's just as we suspected! Unless the audiences are full of City types; in which case, they enjoy the satire because it doesn't hurt; no one in the City *really* acts like that, they reassure themselves. But *Speculators* not only recreates the atmosphere of a foreign exchange dealing room, with all the squalid excitement that naturally entails, it tries to make sense of the characters involved. Why and how could they do these degrading things? it wants to know. And although it tunes into the British public's desire to peer into the private world of the City, it refuses to give it the story it wants to hear. It tries to get behind the City's clamorous money panic. It's funnier than *Serious Money*, it's full of ideas, and it works for real moments of drama rather than limitless frenzy.

Unhappily people don't want any more than *Serious Money* can give them. The characters of *Serious Money* embody a popular confusion. You could also see this in the vogue word 'yuppy' which attached itself – with its ambiguous mixture of distrust, resentment and approval – promiscuously to young City types. You had to hand it to these people, the common perception said: they work long hours, they give it everything, they get paid a lot, they win. They do things that the British haven't done for over a hundred years. They are also coarsely materialistic, pushy and insensitive. Yuppy manages to be a term of abuse, and at the same time, betoken a better, smarter world. It is enough for *Serious Money* to incarnate this mixture of envy and loathing, without getting involved in fiddling realities.

Even a newspaper like *The Sun*, culturally on another planet in comparison with *Serious Money*, fed on City obsession. One day, *The Sun* made it its front-page story. 'Rat Of Blind Date', the headlines said. A commodity broker had appeared on a TV programme called *Blind Date*. This is an entertainment in which Cilla Black uses a game show format to do a little public match-making. The broker told the press how things were run (licentiously, it seemed) backstage. The story could have come from any of *Blind Date*'s oafish contestants, but the commodity broker's City associations, his yuppy status, gave him the edge. It put him on the front page.

We fix our gaze monotonously on the City; the City struggles to confirm that everything is, in fact, going according to plan. There are two acts of faith here. The City tries to believe that it can come to terms with the new world it has somehow embraced; and we grapple with the idea that the City is our new North Sea Oil – a great hidden resource, a thing which brings in money we never thought we'd get. The problem is that while North Sea Oil is inert and unexceptionable, the City is dense with frightful young people, unreconstructed toffs, moral black spots. To think that we owe billions and billions of pounds of revenue to people like the 'Rat Of Blind Date', or to Jake Todd, the doomed toff in *Serious Money* . . .

And what increases our unease, is our certainty that the City doesn't know best how to run itself and yet will fall apart if we tamper with it too much. There's alchemy in the City, which legislators can destroy with one fatuous bill before Parliament. Meddle with us, the City assures us, and no matter how inept we may be now, we will be even worse once you've finished. Despite its evident incompetence, we can have the City, and the wealth it supplies, only on its terms. So when Bryan Gould writes in the *Guardian*, a few months after the crash, about shaping the City to a socialist pattern, his argument, the City says, can never make sense. 'The moral is,' says Bryan Gould, 'we must exercise much more effective influence over the priorities of the City. We shall not be able to do this by public ownership alone ... What we need is a much clearer idea of the role of finance as a servant rather than the master of the real economy ...' But you can't bend the City to a new philosophy. You might as well deal with the authoritarianism of the Roman Catholic Church by abolishing the Pope and requiring cardinals to stand for democratic election. You're left with a new construct that may answer no one's needs. We have to have the money. It doesn't matter that there's this terrible absence of commonality between the City and what Bryan Gould, in orthodox Labour fashion, calls the real economy. We have to forget that, and will ourselves to trust in the City.

The crash did change the nature of this trust. The world's envy now alternates with a kind of hungry condescension. There was an outbreak of gloating in the papers and on the television. 'Dealing Firms A Death Blow', said *The Evening Standard*. 'How Fear Came', chuckled the *Spectator*. Yet we can't afford to mock too strenuously. So here we are locked into a bond of dependence, even though the crash has made the City look even sillier and more dangerous, and even though there are still too many overpaid young men with vulgar habits spending our money for us, tampering with our jobs, calling the shots in ways we couldn't even imagine.

JOKES

And the city is locked into its new world. We look in anxiously at the City, and the City, with increasing nervousness, looks out. The

City likes to make jokes; this is a sign of its nervousness. Some of its jokes are plain yob jokes, jokes made by crass men everywhere. Demon Keith's boss told him this joke, once: 'There are three women applicants for a job as my secretary. The first has five years' experience and good word processing skills. The second has seven years' experience and speaks French. The third is bilingual in English and Japanese, has shorthand, terrific word processing and great references. Which one do I pick? The one with the biggest *jugs!*' It hurts Demon Keith to recount this one, but he recognizes its fatheaded purity. 'I like it,' a stockbroker said. 'It's got plenty of *jissom*'. Here's another: 'Why should you never walk around Kiev with your flies undone? Because *Chernobyl* fall out!' (You have to pronounce *Chernobyl* with the stress on the second syllable for this one to make sense.) Or this one: 'What's the difference between a Eurobond and a Eurobond dealer? A Eurobond matures.'

'These jokes go all around the world,' said a dealer excitedly. 'You post a joke off to Wall Street, it comes back to you via Tokyo. It's the comradeship of the markets.' Other jokes reflect deeper anxieties. 'What's the difference between an equities dealer and a pigeon? A pigeon can still put a deposit on a Porsche.' 'Have you heard, they're doing a deal with Ernest Saunders? They're going to drop the charges, on condition he gets the BP share price up to 330p.' 'Why's it better to have AIDS than a part-paid BP share? Because at least there's a chance of getting rid of AIDS!'

And so on. You make jokes, awful, execrable, offensive, witless jokes, all the time. You share the same imprisonment, while the arbitrary terrors of the money business sweep across your dealing screen or your slag heaps of information. And there's no simple way out, unless your firm sacks you, or you go to prison. The rest of the country is now watching you, the police are watching you, the Securities and Investments Board is watching you, your directors are watching you.

BOESKY AND THE PROBLEM OF KEEPING CLEAN

There don't seem to be that many jokes about Ivan Boesky though. In December, 1987, he was sentenced by Judge Morris Lasker to a three-year prison term. Since he'd already paid over $100m to the Securities and Exchange Commission to settle insider trading charges, Judge Lasker let him off a further fine. Boesky made an impressive plea to the court before sentencing. He said, 'I just want to say that I am deeply ashamed and I do not understand my behaviour. I spent the past year trying to understand how I veered off course. I would like the opportunity as I go forward to redeem myself and leave this earth with a good name. That is what I want.' Boesky, in between grassing to the SEC and implicating the Guinness takeover team, had been doing good works around New York. He had done community service for the cathedral of St John the Divine, under an assumed name. He had given up his stretch limousine in favour of a Subaru coupé. Judge Lasker looked into Boesky's grimy soul and declared, 'I am prepared to believe — maybe I am naive — that he is a reformed individual.'

Just after Christmas, they tried to auction the contents of Boesky's office, the one he had posed in for *Time* magazine all those years before. Around a hundred sensation-seekers squashed together among the tables and chairs. The auctioneer, Michael Amodeo, tried to sell a set of genuine Boesky filing cabinets for no less than $25,000. No one wanted to buy. 'Come on,' Amodeo bellowed, 'there were famous records stored in there.' They went for $750. A wastepaper bin was sold for $5, and someone stole a boxful of Ivan Boesky & Co. headed writing paper.

City people make jokes about Ernest Saunders, because Saunders was a different kind of person. Saunders was a businessman, not a financial professional. But they don't seem to make jokes about Ivan Boesky, or Roger Seelig, or Lord Spens, the merchant banker who was arrested in March 1988. Maybe the prospect of Michael Amodeo tripping across from America to auction off the contents of your hutch, or the shreds of personal existence from the battery pen where you lived, is too painful. Maybe it's the similarity between bankruptcy and death which makes it hard to laugh off.

City people aren't monsters. They generally don't devote their working lives to a scam, like Boesky, or Dennis Levine. But they do live in a cloud of dangerous knowledge. Often, there is no difference between insider information and information you merely happen to get before anyone else. Circumstance decides which it might be. So what do you do? Insider trading has been called, wonderfully, the victimless crime. As J. K. Galbraith observes about embezzlement, for the period in which the embezzler has his gain, and in which the person who has been embezzled is unaware of his loss, there is an overall increase in psychic wealth. Insider trading nearly fits this description. The final loss suffered by the company shareholders who aren't insider dealing is so hard to quantify that there might as well be no loss at all. The fact is, though, that one person has used his position to the disadvantage of others. It's no less fraudulent than the crime of using a computer to thieve minute percentages from bank accounts. The wrong is still there, an outsider will argue, even if it's painless.

But in the City, you can talk about the victimless crime. You can dabble with this sordid contradiction in terms. City people work to increase the wealth of their clients. That's the fundamental good. Does it make you a bad person if that's the fundamental good of your working life? Well, not bad — just different. City people work with the essences of capitalism. The City is a home to the international capitalist impulse stripped bare, the elemental force of money which races around the world from Tokyo to London to New York. If you're against the City, then you are against capitalism itself. You can't be bothered with domestic scruples in the face of the spirit of international capitalism. Some people go too far, it's true. But the rest of the City, it understands that this force of money compels you, as in a war, to shelve that everyday part of yourself which contributes to Oxfam and goes to church, and worries about discipline in your child's school.

Lucky Paul, Webb, the Ace Merchant Banker: these aren't *bad* people — just, different. The Financial Services Act and the Securities and Investment Board and the DTI have to recognize that different standards apply. Go to Riyadh; go to Bangkok; go to Leningrad: different standards apply there. That's what you expect. There is no fixed global morality. You borrow your moral expectations from the person next to you. The City upholds the standards of international capitalism. Dammit, blurts out the City Old Boy, we have enough on our hands working the battery pens and saving our multinational money combines from bleeding to death after the crash. We have plenty to do, just coping with the elemental force of money when it goes mad; we have to cope with this *thing*. And we still have the Yankees and the Japanese breathing in our faces. We don't have the time for rules.

THE AMERICAN

After all the sackings, and the myth of The World's Least Sympathetic Humans, and the general distaste with which non-Americans viewed Americans in the City, you might expect the American to be chastened in his approach to things. Many people are prone to dismiss Salomon's, Shearson Lehman, Citicorp and the rest, as Yankee buffoons. They hate them for the rapacity they encouraged as the City set itself up for Big Bang. They persuade one another to despise the Americans for their attitudes towards client relationships. Popularly, the Yankees are thought to have one tactic; get in there, sell the guy what he wants at the lowest price – we have the *muscle* to do this – and then get out. He wants something else next year? Sure. He can call us any time. They are tainted with the crash mentality, and the furious incontinence of the Great Glutton. Does all this bother the American? Not for a moment.

'*Right*,' he argues, 'we have to work on our *intrapersonal* skills. *Right*. It's something we *neglected*. It's something you need in Europe. You have to have it. But all this stuff about *retrenchment* and *losses* and pulling back from the global market – this is *bullshit*!' He actually says *bullshit!*, and jabs the air with his index finger.

The American works for a huge American bank. He has been in London for the last four years. He seems to like it. 'It's more relaxed than New York. It's more civilized. You have the art galleries and the theatre and the opera. Paris is nice too. But the fucking *French*!

172

What a bunch of assholes! But I like being in Europe.' More than any European, he has this broad conception of the EC as one state, where anyone who counts speaks English, and where credit cards are widely accepted.

'What we're doing now, is *rationalizing*. I think we pitched into too many things at once in the early 1980s. I think everybody did. We know that. So now we're consolidating our strengths and building up at the points we're weak.' He is absolutely confident in this. Nothing can stop his Yankee multinational from doing what it wants to. How could anything stop it? They may not have as much money as the Japanese, but they're still bloated with capital. 'I mean, take a look at some of the deals that are happening. The government of Italy wants to make a billion dollar bond issue? Right? Now, who is going to be big enough to service that kind of issue? Who has the capital to underwrite that kind of thing? I mean, the Japs, they have the money, right, but they're not *developed*. So you go to one of the little traditional British merchant banks? How *could* they do a deal like that? Hambros, Barings, they've got a few hundred million, maybe. They could syndicate a deal, but why do that when you can go to us! We have the capital resources, we have the expertise, we have the presence in the market, we can take the *whole thing* on, like *that!*'

He's right. People like Hambros and Barings grew up in a tradition of domestic business, of quiet ties with small British companies. They haven't got the money for a gargantuan bond issue, or vast equity flotation. They have to parcel the thing out and split the various commissions, and slowly put a package together.

Indeed, The American's instinct is to calumniate the little British merchant banks until his face turns blue. Perhaps he's spent too much time in too many meetings, suffering their condescension. In American terms, he's a patrician; Harvard first degree, Harvard MBA straight after that, a family of gravelly professionals behind him, a cheerful familiarity with the English and their ways. But under the gaze of some stifling Lazards toff, he's still a Yankee with a pro-nounced New Yorker's snarl in his voice. How could he resist taking a kick at the little British merchant bankers? 'I don't,' he says, '*respect* them.

'Some of them are okay, but frankly, some of them are *assholes*. Truly, *assholes*. They can be a bunch of lazy *bullshitters*. That's true. They sit on their asses, 'cause they know they're getting paid a fortune, and the quality of work they do is *shit*.' He gets more excited as he sketches in the catastrophe. 'They have very little capital, they can make perhaps one – two – deals a year, and provide some kind of special service to their old clients; but they're *out of touch*. There is no way they can live in the same market place as a Salomon or a Nomura. Even someone like Kleinwort Benson, someone big in British terms, they're going to be *nowhere*. We are going to walk all over them. We've been through the first wave of expansion in the first half of the 1980s. We know what our strengths and weaknesses are more clearly. We're learning *all the time* about building better client relationships. How *can* they compete? In five years' time it's going to be us, the Japanese, maybe Warburgs and BZW. The little guys are *finished!*'

He leans right over the table. He is pure, vulcanized American. All the sneering at the hysterical Salomons and Shearson Lehmans must be getting to him. He wants you to know that whatever happened in 1987, the Americans can still beat the crap out of you, whenever they feel like it. Where does he learn all this stuff? Harvard Business school? The Yankee multinational?

'Right. We can be too aggressive, at times,' he admits, subsiding into his chair. He smoothes down his thick, greying hair. He has wrong-footed himself. You can see the house policy running through his mind: If we're going to stay with these people, we must build good relationships. We must be diplomatic. 'No, I mean, some of these little firms can be very good, *excellent* at what they do. I can see some of them settling in as specialists, niche houses, providing a very good, custom-made service in one or two specialist areas. There's just going to be a shake-up in between now and then. I mean, we can work with them. They can fit in with us . . .' But he has to take another kick; it's a compulsion. 'All it is, is that *I* expect nothing less than total commitment from the people who work with me. They know that if they don't deliver, they're out. That's how I do it. So when I see these *bullshitters* in some merchant banks, I just don't have any *respect* for them. They should not be there. They're going to be *caught out* ... Some of them are very good – some of them are *assholes*. We *know* how much better we are at corporate finance, merchant banking, managing issues, debt structuring. Some of them are assholes ...'

He is confused. Four years in Europe, and he still comes out with this hectic, ball-breaking stuff. Really, he doesn't believe the house policy on diplomatic relationships. He knows that, in five years' time, it'll all be down to the Americans and the Japanese. BZW, Warburgs, they might have the professional nuts to get into the new age, but the rest are dying already. Who needs this diplomacy? We're talking about professionalism.

And then, there are still the Japanese. The American doesn't respect the Japanese, but he does fear them. 'They have got *so much* capital – it's awesome ...' And the Japanese have only just begun.

THE MAN FROM NOMURA

The Nomura Group are like the rest of the post-war Japanese economy: relentless. In 1964, they had an office in London, staffed by three Japanese guys. It was called a 'pillar box' for the rest of the organization. Now, in the late 1980s, there are over six hundred people working in Nomura's pallid office block next to the Monument, of whom 90 per cent are British. The firm started in Osaka, in 1872. Now it has thirty-four offices in twenty countries; it has the world's biggest in-house financial research organization, at the Nomura Research Institute (which employs more than 650 people); it is one of only three firms with membership of the London, New York and Tokyo Stock Exchanges, and it is the biggest securities house in the world.

The Finance King has had dealings with the Japanese. 'The Japanese,' he claims, 'are playing the game completely differently. It's not even the same game. They're not even on the same *planet*. They don't worry about making a profit now, or next year, or even fifteen years from now. They say, well, if we make a profit twenty years from now, that's good. They just don't give a shit about anyone else. Nomura,' he concedes, stiffly, 'are different from most Japs. They make an effort to fit in. But the other Jap firms; they do deals only in Japanese shares – they make deals interhouse where not a single word of English is spoken.'

'The important thing for us at the moment, is the concept of *dochaku-ka*, which means "fitting into the woodwork",' says the Man From Nomura, lighting up a Rothmans in his office. This is the sort of room you thought the Ace Merchant Banker might have justified. It is done up in a traditional Corporate Bastard Yankee style, with doom-laden woodwork, a pervert's chair covered with black leather and bronze studs, and a monstrous bare desk for the Man From Nomura to sit behind. The only object which hints at the true home of the Man From Nomura is a glass case about four feet high, standing in the corner, and containing a little model of a *geisha*. 'With *dochaku-ka*, working for Nomura is really like working for a local firm. But with some differences.'

One difference, according to spiteful outsiders, is that *everything* has to be checked by head office in Tokyo, before it can be implemented. According to a brooding merchant banker, 'The fax machine is on *all night*.'

'Yes. Decision making is a very lengthy process. We involve all people, from London, New York and Tokyo. You see, we are under pressure to reach the *area* we want, but our time deadline is much longer. To quote our managing director: "The absence of pressures means you can do small things well."' To whom is he referring? Presumably Nomura's new chief, Yoshihisa Tabuchi. Tabuchi is pictured in the promotional books, gazing shrewdly out at you, and holding a newspaper whose headline reads: 'Watch The Traitors Run'.

Traitors, for Nomura, are people who make things bad for the team. 'We look, not for shining superstars, but for team players. We want to build our staff and mould them into a *team*. And the worst thing that you could do, is *walk away from the team*.' The Man From Nomura lights up another Rothmans. Tabuchi chainsmokes too. Perhaps it is now company policy to chainsmoke. 'We take people who are basically team individuals. We did get one guy from Citibank on swaps who was *a real individual* – but he couldn't last.'

The Man From Nomura has a difficult job. Like The American
and his fumblings with diplomacy, the Man From Nomura's clinging
to *dochaku-ka* begins to sound increasingly fainthearted. You fit in,
in Nomura. There are no bourgeois individualists, western style. It is
said that the sense of hierarchy at Nomura is so conscientious, that
you cannot be appointed to a position inferior to anyone who is
younger than you are. It is also said that your job requires you to
unwind in public bars long after the Lucky Pauls and the Ace Merchant Bankers have gone home to their women and *Newsnight*. 'This
is largely true,' agrees the Man From Nomura. 'You do go to bars
after work. The objective is to relax and get to know your colleagues. Many people also play *mah-jongg*. It's a useful way of understanding the person you're playing with. It's also very competitive . . .'

The *team* embodies a fierce and vigorous compromise. The team
isn't just a group of men doing the same thing; it is a subsuming of
personal energy into a corporate act. You have, it seems, to be
ruthlessly keen and yet without ego. Your self-aggrandisement —
the force behind Seelig, Posgate, even Lucky Paul — must become
the aggrandisement of Nomura. And when you let go in the
evenings, you let go competitively but corporately at the same
time. All competition lies within the grid of Nomura's ambitions.
Even in the singing bars.

There are *karaoke* clubs in London: Japanese pubs where you get
drunk, and then, one by one, step up on to a podium to sing along
with a professionally-produced pop backing track. You sing 'Yes-
terday', 'Dreaming', 'Tie A Yellow Ribbon', 'Walking On The Moon'.
It is unlikely you will get the chance to do 'Cold Turkey', or 'Subterranean Homesick Blues'. The 90 per cent indigenous staff at
Nomura's London office haven't really got the feel for the *karaoke*
clubs yet, but the Japanese staff can't live without them. 'They're
very competitive about it. They use professional backing tracks and
they take it very seriously. Some of them are actually very good
singers.'

This kind of thing doubles back on the Man From Nomura, who
finds himself caressingly discussing *dochaku-ka* at one moment, and
the fantastical business of the *karaoke* clubs the next. He wrestles
with the contradictions, light up another Rothmans, smiles feebly. It

177

also fuddles people outside Nomura's culture. The British, supposedly, find the Japanese more sympathetic to deal with than the
Yankees, because of their formality, their sense of hierarchy, their
caution. They're tractable, say the City Old Boys. They're also
faintly ludicrous. They have this Mount Fujiyama of capital, but
they don't know what to do with it. They take forever to reach
decisions; their techniques are, let's face it, crass. The City contents
itself with this thought. It quells the nervousness which it feels at
the prospect of Nomura's (not to mention Daiwa's, Dai-Ichi's,
Sumitomo's, or Nikko's) riches. They're *crass*. They might make cars
and televisions, but they won't be bankers and brokers to the world.
How can you talk to someone who spends his evenings drinking
Chivas Regal and crooning to a tape of 'Sailing'?

But then, the Japanese used to make crass cars. Remember the
Nissan Cedric? They just worked diligently through the crassness
until they reached the point where Japanese goods are now thought
of as premium purchases. The *karaoke* clubs, the pensiveness, the
obstinate cult of the team – these can lead the City astray. Silly
Japs! They need us more than we need them!

But the Man From Nomura roots around in his Rothmans packet,
digs out the last one and lights it. 'We take the long-term view. We
select our staff carefully. We do things in small stages, but we try to
do them well. We've recently opened a banking division to com-
plement the securities operation. It's small at the moment, but it's a
start. That's how we like to do things. Carefully, but well.' The Man
From Nomura sits back. He knows that Nomura will be with us for
a long time. He has no problems with *dochakuk-ka*, the fax machine
that chatters away all night, the irresistible hierarchy. And the Man
From Nomura is English.

THE SUMP OF OBSESSIONS

Wealth, competition, success. How strange these things sound in
daunted Britain; but the City clings to them. It has a dream – the
City of London, Wall Street, Tokyo, the imperial powers of finance,

the money triumvirate. It struggles with a mixture of the most familiar British obsessions: class and meritocracy; the fear of technology; cunning foreigners; efficiency and sloth; the notion of extravagant reward; sharp practice; the gloomy horror of yet another British failure.

They're all there, in the perfect City, these terrible preoccupations. And the more we know about the place, the greater our spiritual, as well as financial, investment in it. We have to trust in whatever comes out of this chaos of change, and believe in the confidence trick. Half a million people are trying to master the spirit of international capitalism before the next crash. Half a million people are trying to prove that the British really can make it against the Americans and the Japanese — that for once, they won't destroy us and our lingering ambitions.

We've invested billions, say the City firms. We've got the best people working for us. We're looking towards the future with justifiable confidence. But under their breath, they repeat the motto of the City of London, the prayer which underlines the City's dragons: *Domine Dirige Nos.*